National 4 & 5
HOSPITALITY
COURSE NOTES

Edna Hepburn • Lynn Smith

N4 & 5 HOSPITALITY
COURSE NOTES

001/20022014

10 9 8 7 6 5 4 3 2 1

ISBN 9780007504817

Published by
Leckie & Leckie Ltd
An imprint of HarperCollins*Publishers*
Westerhill Road, Bishopbriggs, Glasgow, G64 2QT
T: 0844 576 8126 F: 0844 576 8131
leckieandleckie@harpercollins.co.uk   www.leckieandleckie.co.uk

Special thanks to
Donna Cole (copy edit); Roda Morrison (proofread);
Sonia Dawkins (proofread) Ink Tank (cover design); Jouve (layout)

Printed in Italy by Lego, S.P.A.

A CIP Catalogue record for this book is available from the British Library.

Acknowledgements
P34 (knives) licensed under the Creative Commons Attribution-Share Alike 3.0 Unported license, P36 (vegetable peelers) licensed under the Creative Commons Attribution-Share Alike 3.0 Unported license, P40 (graters) licensed under the Creative Commons Attribution-Share Alike 3.0 Unported license, P42 (ball whisk) licensed under the Creative Commons Attribution-Share Alike 3.0 Unported license, P48 (julienne peeler) licensed under the Creative Commons Attribution-Share Alike 3.0 Unported license

All other images © Shutterstock.com

*Recipes for all Service chef activities are available to download, **free**, from the Leckie and Leckie website. Go to **www.leckieandleckie.co.uk/n45hospitality***

Introduction

Starter for 10 – the countdown

Countdown for
10 ... 9 ... 8 ... 7 ... 6 ... 5 ... 4 ... 3 ... 2 ... 1 ...

10: What's this course all about?

The chapters in this book cover the three units of the course.

1. Cookery Skills, Techniques and Processes.
2. Understanding and Using Ingredients.
3. Organisational Skills for Cooking.

At the start of each unit you will find:

- a short description of the unit.
- the two outcomes (what you have to do).
- what you have to know or do to pass each Outcome of the unit (the Assessment Standards).

How are the units assessed?

Each of the Outcomes and Assessment Standards in the units has to be assessed. This can be done in two ways:

1. Unit-by-unit assessment – this means that each unit is assessed separately.
2. Portfolio of assessment – this means that each assessment standard is assessed separately.
3. Combined assessment – this means that either two or three units can be combined and assessed together.

Course assessment

After you have completed the three units, you will have the opportunity to do the Course assessment.

The National 5 Course assessment is a practical activity undertaken under controlled conditions. The practical activity is set by the SQA and is worth 100 marks.

You will have to plan, produce and serve the three given recipes for four people within 2 hours 30 minutes. Useful information which will help you do well in your practical activity is found in chapter 7.

The National 4 Added Value Unit is also a practical activity. You will have to follow a given time plan to prepare, cook and serve a two-course meal.

Other features of the book

✓ Chef's test

These are short questions which will test your knowledge.

👨‍🍳 Service chef!

These are suggestions of practical activities you can try out. Recipes for all of the dishes suggested are available to download, **free**, from the leckie and leckie website! Go to www.leckieandleckie.co.uk/n45hospitality

GO! Activities

These are activities that will allow you to reinforce your knowledge through practical food preparation tasks, challenges, problem solving activities while working on your own, in pairs or in groups.

❓ Did you know?

Additional facts about a topic to engage further interest and to bring the subject to life.

📁 Portfolio

Portfolio of work – this indicates a piece of work that could be placed in your portfolio of evidence.

🔍 Hint

Give helpful tips and highlight important information.

Rate your progress – this gives you an opportunity to rate how confident you are in understanding the topics within the chapter. You can also identify your 'next steps' to improving your work.

Countdown for

10 ... **9** ... 8 ... 7 ... 6 ... 5 ... 4 ... 3 ... 2 ... 1 ...

9: Get prepared

Start you day in the right way by carrying out the following steps:

Step 1: Clean up your act!

Personal hygiene is of paramount importance when working in a kitchen. It is therefore important that you carry out the following before turning up for work:

1. Have a shower/bath.
2. Tie long hair up securely.
3. Remove any nail varnish and trim fingernails – they should be short and clean.
4. Remove any body piercings.
5. Males should be cleanly shaven.
6. No jewellery, including wedding rings.

Step 2: Get into gear!

1. Make sure you have all of your uniform for the day and that it is clean and neatly pressed.
2. Make sure shoes are polished, no traces of the previous day's cooking!

Hat

Necktie

Chef's jacket

Apron

Chef's trousers

Non-slip footwear, preferably with a steel toe cap

Step 3: Sharpen those tools!
Knives should be sharpened before turning up for work and they should be clean and in the right carry case.

Step 4: Time for the right mind-set!
Uniform helps you to get into the correct frame of mind for the day, however the following '**Employability skills**' are definitely the key to getting on in the hospitality industry:

Ask the chef de cuisine

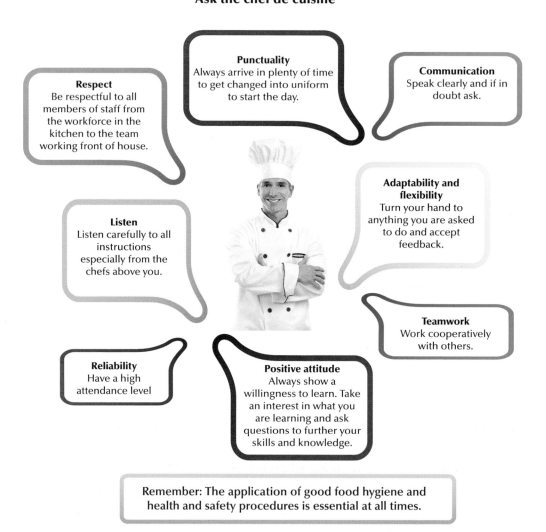

Respect
Be respectful to all members of staff from the workforce in the kitchen to the team working front of house.

Punctuality
Always arrive in plenty of time to get changed into uniform to start the day.

Communication
Speak clearly and if in doubt ask.

Listen
Listen carefully to all instructions especially from the chefs above you.

Adaptability and flexibility
Turn your hand to anything you are asked to do and accept feedback.

Teamwork
Work cooperatively with others.

Reliability
Have a high attendance level

Positive attitude
Always show a willingness to learn. Take an interest in what you are learning and ask questions to further your skills and knowledge.

Remember: The application of good food hygiene and health and safety procedures is essential at all times.

🔍 Hint

Carry a small notebook and pen in your pocket and make notes about techniques/ recipes as you go through the day and always reflect on your performance at the end of each day.

✔ Chef's test

Complete the following:

1. Make up an advice sheet about 'being prepared' to give to a student wishing to become a chef.
2. Use the Internet to find out more information on what you need to do if you wish to take up a career in the hospitality industry.

Countdown for

10 ... 9 ... **8** ... 7 ... 6 ... 5 ... 4 ... 3 ... 2 ... 1 ...

8: How to become a rising star

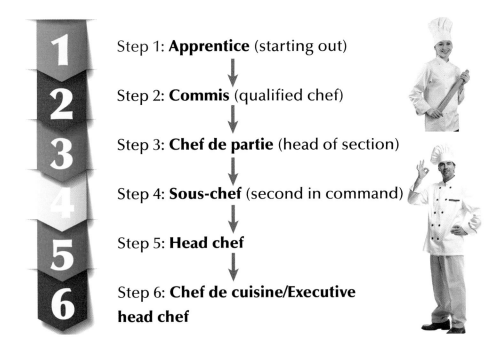

Step 1: **Apprentice** (starting out)

Step 2: **Commis** (qualified chef)

Step 3: **Chef de partie** (head of section)

Step 4: **Sous-chef** (second in command)

Step 5: **Head chef**

Step 6: **Chef de cuisine/Executive head chef**

An '**apprentice**' is just starting out a career in the hospitality industry. They spend their time going between the college and working in an establishment.

A **commis** is a basic chef in larger kitchens who works under a chef de partie to learn the responsibilities and operation of a station.

A **chef de partie** may also be known as a 'station chef' and is in charge of a particular area of production. In large kitchens, each station chef might have several assistants such as apprentices and commis, however, in most kitchens the station chef is the only worker in that section.

The '**sous-chef**' (under-chef of the kitchen) is the second in command and direct assistant of the head chef. The roles of this chef include:

a) Scheduling and substituting when the head chef is off-duty.
b) Filling in for or assisting the chef de partie when needed.
c) The responsibility for the inventory, cleanliness of the kitchen, organisation and training of all employees.

Smaller kitchens may not have a sous-chef, while larger kitchens may have several.

'**Chef de cuisine**' and **Executive Head Chef**. This person is in charge of all things related to the kitchen including:

a) Menu creation.
b) Management of kitchen staff.
c) Hygiene procedures.
d) Ordering and purchasing of inventory.
e) Plating design of dishes.

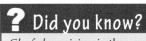 **Did you know?**

Chef de cuisine is the traditional French term from which the English word chef is derived.

Work your way through the sections

Below are the main sections found in every kitchen, however, the number of staff within each section can vary depending on the size of kitchen and grade of cuisine.

Section	English title	French title	Description
Meat section	roast chef	*rôtisseur*	Prepares roasted and braised meats and their appropriate sauce.
	grill chef	*grillardin*	Prepares all grilled foods.
	butcher	*boucher*	Butchers meats, poultry and fish.
Fish section	fish chef	*poissonnier*	Prepares fish dishes and often does all fish butchering as well as appropriate sauces.
Garnish section	garnish chef	*entremetier*	Prepares hot appetisers and often prepares the soups, vegetables, pastas and starches. Prepares all hot garnishes.
Larder section	larder chef	*garde manger*	Responsible for preparing cold foods, including salads, cold appetizers, *pâtés* and other *charcuterie* items.
Pastry section	pastry chef	*pâtissier*	Is qualified in making baked goods such as pastries, cakes, biscuits, macaroons, chocolates, breads and desserts. Pastry chefs can specialise in cakes in patisseries or bakeries by making cupcakes, wedding cakes, birthday and special occasion cakes.

? Did you know?

In larger establishments, the pastry chef often supervises a separate team in their own kitchen or separate work area.

✔ Chef's test

Complete the following:

1. Name the highest rank of chef and state what they are responsible for.
2. Describe the role of a sous-chef.
3. Name the main sections in a professional kitchen.

Countdown for

10 ... 9 ... 8 ... **7** ... 6 ... 5 ... 4 ... 3 ... 2 ... 1 ...

7: Prevention is better than cure

When working in the hospitality industry, it is a legal requirement to ensure that:

- All food served is fit for human consumption.
- Premises are clean and in a good state of repair.

Failure to carry out these simple rules can lead to a criminal conviction, which can result in a fine or a jail sentence.

Keeping on the right side of the law

Safe and hygienic food practices, whether at home or in the hospitality industry, should be the same to prevent outbreaks of food poisoning.

The following food preparation rules should apply throughout.

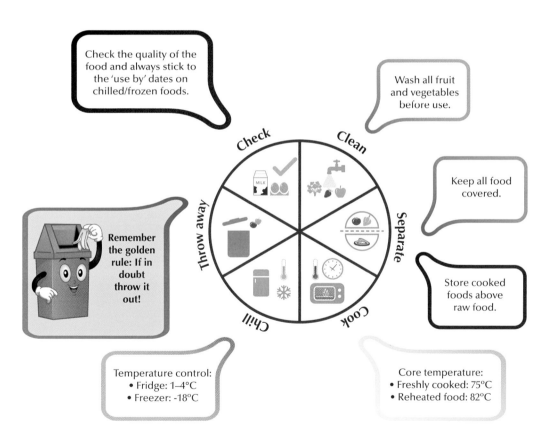

Your responsibility	
DOs	**DON'Ts**
• Wash hands after going to the toilet and before and after touching raw food – this will prevent bacteria being transferred to food. • Cover any cuts/boils with a blue waterproof plaster to prevent bacterial contamination of the food. Blue food gloves may also be used. • Tie hair back to prevent it landing on the food. Wear clean protective clothing to protect the food from you!	• Don't wear jewellery or have visible body piercings as they harbour bacteria. • Don't smoke as fingers touch the lips then the food, resulting in contamination. • Don't wear strong perfume – it taints the food. • Don't cough or sneeze over food – the mouth, nose or ears all contain bacteria. • Don't 'double dip' spoons when tasting food as this can contaminate the food. • Don't wear nail varnish or false nails, as these could flake or fall off into the food.

Hazard analysis critical control point (HACCP) – Q&A

1. **Question:** What is HACCP?

   Answer: It is a system that has been developed to check food safety from the start to the finish of the food chain.

2. **Question:** Who has to follow the HACCP system?

   Answer: Food service providers such as restaurants, hotels, fast food chains, school canteens, hospitals, care homes and mobile caterers.

3. **Question:** What are the benefits of the HACCP system for the hospitality industry?

   Answer:

   a) Hazards are identified at each stage of the food preparation and controls are put in place to prevent bacterial growth and food poisoning.

   b) Businesses will build up a good reputation and customers will want to return.

   c) There will be a reduction in complaints and negative publicity.

   d) It stops the business breaking the food laws.

4. **Question:** How does the HACCP system work?

   Answer: There are seven stages involved in the HACCP system.

Stage 1 – Conduct a hazard analysis

This is where any hazards that must be avoided, removed or reduced are identifed. Possible hazards in the hospitality industry include:

1. **Contamination:**
   - **Biological** such as bacteria, moulds and viruses.
   - **Chemical** such as cleaning chemicals and pesticides.
   - **Physical** such as foreign bodies like glass, pests, metal.
2. **Temperature control during storage** – bacteria and mould will multiply if stored at a higher temperature than recommended.
3. **Insufficient cooking** – can lead to bacteria surviving.

Stage 2 – Decide on the critical control points

A **control point** is when a hazard does not carry a food poisoning risk and therefore good hygiene practices at this stage should be sufficient to ensure food safety.

Critical control points are the points where you need to prevent, remove or reduce the hazard to prevent the risk of food poisoning. (For example temperature control with a high-risk food such as chicken.)

Stage 3 – Establish a tolerance level

The controls must be applied at this stage to eliminate the hazard or reduce it to a safe level. For example, for a cooked food this might include setting the minimum cooking temperature and time required to ensure food poisoning bacteria are destroyed.

Stage 4 – Establish a monitoring system

This stage involves checking to make sure that the controls put in place are being carried out and are working effectively. Time and temperature are two very important controls that are relatively easy to monitor, such as refrigerator and freezer temperatures being checked and the temperature noted at set times in the day.

Stage 5 – Establish what action could be taken to correct the hazard if it occurs

This is where corrective action has to take place if a problem has been identified through the monitoring system or a complaint has been received. Some examples of corrective action include:

- Disposing of food if the minimum cooking temperature has not been met.
- Throwing out any stock that is out of date.

Stage 6 – Establish procedures to check that the HACCP system works effectively

An example of this could be testing a time and temperature recording device to prove that a piece of equipment is working properly.

Stage 7 – Record keeping and review of procedures

This is where records are kept of any identified hazards, controls put in place and the monitoring that has taken place. It is a **legal requirement** to keep records of procedures followed. These records will be used as evidence to show '**due diligence**' in the event of a prosecution.

'**Due diligence**' means that the business can prove that they have taken all reasonable precautions to avoid committing an offence.

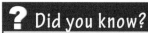

? Did you know?

If you are planning to start a new catering business, you must register your premises with the Environmental Health Service at your local authority at least 28 days before opening.

5. **Question:** At what points does the HACCP system have to be applied?

   Answer: The areas where HACCP must be used in the hospitality industry are:

   - delivery/purchase of ingredients
   - storage of ingredients
   - preparation of ingredients
   - cooking of ingredients
   - chilled storage/cooling
   - serving of food

6. **Question:** Who are Environmental Health Officers?

   Answer: These are people who are employed by the government to protect public health.

7. **Question:** What is the role of Environmental Health Officers (EHOs) in the hospitality industry?

   Answer: They inspect food premises to make sure they are operating hygienically and are not a risk to public health. They handle complaints about food quality, hygiene and safety issues.

8. **Question:** What powers do EHOs have?

    Answer: Where they inspect a food premises and identify any potential risks they can:

    a) Serve an improvement notice with a time scale for the work to be carried out.
    b) Seize foods samples and send them for testing.
    c) Serve an immediate closure notice.

✔ Chef's test

Complete the following:

1. Make up a help sheet about setting up HACCP for someone wanting to open a new restaurant.
2. What is the role of Environmental Health Officers and what powers do they have?

Countdown for

10 ... 9 ... 8 ... 7 ... **6** ... 5 ... 4 ... 3 ... 2 ... 1 ...

6: Keeping the bugs at bay

As a food handler you have an important role to play in preventing food becoming contaminated by micro-organisms (bacteria, moulds, yeasts and viruses). There are various terms you will come across as you handle food.

Confused? – Don't be

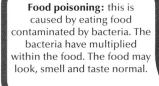

Food poisoning: this is caused by eating food contaminated by bacteria. The bacteria have multiplied within the food. The food may look, smell and taste normal.

Cross-contamination: this happens when bacteria are transferred from their sources to a cooked food.

Food spoilage: this is when food 'goes off'. The smell, taste and look of the food make it unfit to eat and should be thrown away.

Food-borne disease: this is caused by eating food which is contaminated by micro-organisms. These then multiply within the body and cause illness.

There are **two ways** that we can cross contaminate.

1. **Direct contamination.** Bacteria go directly from the source to the food. Some examples are:

   - coughing onto food
   - a fly landing on food
   - blood from raw meat dripping onto the cooked meat below in a fridge.

2. **Indirect contamination.** Bacteria are transferred to the food with some help, e.g. from our hands, equipment, cloths, work surfaces. These are known as "**vehicles of contamination**." Some examples are:

   - licking fingers then handling food
   - using the same chopping board or knife for raw then cooked food
   - using the same cloth after wiping a raw food area to wipe a cooked food area.

What are your responsibilities as a food handler?
As a food handler you must handle and serve food safely and hygienically. Failure to do this can result in the following:

- Outbreaks of food poisoning, which can be serious and can cause death especially in children and elderly people.
- Bad publicity and loss of a good reputation.
- Closure of food premises.

You must not handle food if you have any of the following symptoms – sickness, diarrhoea, fever, abdominal pain. You must be clear of any symptoms for at least 24 hours before returning to work and all incidents of illness must be reported to your supervisor as this is a legal requirement.

Micro-organisms

- **Bacteria:** Bacteria are the main cause of food poisoning and food-borne illness, and a cause of food spoilage. Some are harmless but the ones that cause food poisoning are called **pathogenic** bacteria.

- **Spores:** Some bacteria form spores. This is a resistant resting phase of the bacteria which protects them against adverse conditions such as the high temperatures of cooking, the cold (by freezing) and by chemicals. Spores do not multiply but as soon as favourable conditions exist, e.g. warmth, they release the bacteria, which then start to multiply.

- **Toxins:** Several bacteria produce toxins (poisons) within the food itself or in the body and this causes illness. Some toxins cannot be destroyed by normal cooking and so are extremely dangerous.

Common food poisoning bacteria

Clostridium perfringens
Sources: raw meat, poultry and their products, carrots and potatoes. Toxins are produced in the food. Food should not be cooked too far in advance of service and should be correctly cooked and then refrigerated until needed.

Staphylococcus aureus
Sources: you (the staff)! Skin, nose, throat, hair, cuts. Good personal hygiene is essential.

Salmonella
Sources: raw meat, poultry and eggs, raw unwashed vegetables, vermin and pets.

Bacillus cereus
Sources: mainly rice dishes, especially if these have not been cooled quickly after cooking. As toxins are produced, do not reheat left-over rice as this can lead to toxins being produced which can result in food poisoning.

Clostridium botulinum
Sources: canned or vacuum-packed foods. These bacteria produce spores that resist methods such as canning. Avoid dented tins. A toxin is produced that can cause paralysis and death.

Food-borne disease-causing bacteria

Listeria
Sources: chilled or cook-chill products, e.g. prepared salads, pâté, soft cheeses, ready meals. Cook-chill products should not be eaten after the 'use by' date and reheated ready meals should reach a centre temperature of 82°C.

E Coli 0157
Sources: Raw and undercooked beef and chicken products e.g. beefburgers, barbequed foods, raw vegetables, unpasteurised milk. All meat should be cooked until the juices run clear. This type of food poisoning can cause kidney failure and death.

Campylobacter
Sources: raw and undercooked meat and poultry, contaminated milk and water. Contamination usually occurs from excrement of birds and animals.

? **Did you know?**

Listeria is particularly dangerous for pregnant women as the unborn baby can be harmed.

What conditions do bacteria need to grow?

1. Food

Bacteria need food to survive and some foods allow bacteria to grow quickly.

	Foods
High-risk foods are potentially hazardous foods	• Eggs and egg products • Cooked rice and cooked or fresh pasta • Raw and cooked meats • Poultry • Fish and shellfish • Stews, soups and stocks • Sauces and gravies • Milk and dairy products such as cream and cheese • Pizza, sandwiches and filled cakes
Low-risk foods are those in which bacteria don't grow well	• Dried – flour, fruit, sugar • Frozen – but bacteria will start to grow as the food defrosts • High in acid – pickles, chutneys • High in fat, salt and sugar

2. Temperature

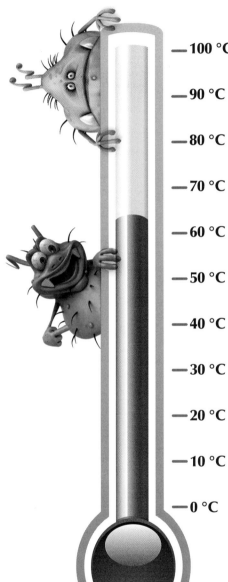

—100 °C

—90 °C

—80 °C

—70 °C

—60 °C

—50 °C

—40 °C

—30 °C

—20 °C

—10 °C

—0 °C

DEATH TO BACTERIA!
In boiling water (100°C) most bacteria die.

82°C – reheated food should reach this temperature.

75°C – this is the core temperature. Cooking food until this temperature (or above) is reached will ensure that harmful bacteria are destroyed.

63°C – this is the minimum 'hot holding' temperature for foods that are to be sold as hot food.

FUN TIME FOR BACTERIA!
37°C – bacteria like the warmth and prefer to live at body temperature. At this temperature they will grow and multiply at their fastest rate.

DANGER ZONE!
This is the temperature between 5° and 63°C and is the temperature at which bacteria rapidly multiply. Foods should only be in the danger zone for as short a time as possible.

SLOW DOWN!
Low temperatures of 1–4°C (the normal temperature of a fridge) will slow the growth of most bacteria but does not kill them.

SNOOZE TIME!
Very low temperatures –18°C (the normal temperature of a freezer) will ensure the bacteria become dormant or sleepy in frozen food. However as food starts to thaw bacteria will become active again.

? Did you know?

It is recommended that hot food is quickly cooled to below 10°C within 1.5 hours. The maximum size for a joint of meat is 2.5 kg. If the joint of meat is any larger then it would be difficult to cool to 10°C within the time.

? Did you know?

Meats have a neutral pH and bacteria are much more likely to multiply therefore greater care must be taken during food preparation.

? Did you know?

Not all bacteria, yeasts and mould are dangerous. Bacteria are used in yoghurt making. Yeasts are used in the making of bread. Mould are used in the ripening of some cheeses e.g. Blue Stilton

? Did you know?

After you remove a joint of meat from an oven, allow it to rest for the **amount of time stated in the recipe**, as it will continue to cook due to the high temperature. It is **important not to go over the stated resting time**, as the temperature will drop into the **danger zone**.

3. Time

Given the correct conditions, bacteria can divide in two every 10–20 minutes. This process is called '**binary fission**'. This means that in 3.5 hours, one bacterium can become one million.

4. Moisture

Bacteria need moisture to grow. When dried food is mixed with water, e.g. dried milk, then bacterial growth will start as these foods become high-risk and need to be stored appropriately.

5. pH

The pH scale measures the acidity or alkalinity of a substance. In general, bacteria cannot grow in conditions that are too acidic or too alkaline:

- A pH of 0-6 is acidic. Acid conditions, e.g. vinegar, will prevent bacteria from growing.
- A pH of 7 is neutral. Most bacteria will grow well at pH 7.
- A pH of 8–14 is alkaline. Bacteria will grow in these conditions.

6. Oxygen

Most bacteria need oxygen to grow, and are known as **aerobic** bacteria. However, some bacteria can grow without oxygen, and are called **anaerobic** bacteria.

Moulds

Mould is a microscopic plant or fungi that may appear as fluffy looking patches on foods like jam, cheese and bread. Many moulds spoil food and can cause illness in humans by producing toxins. Mouldy food should always be thrown out – never just cut off the mouldy patch because mould can travel up to 2 cm within the food and be invisible to the eye.

Yeasts

A yeast is a type of fungus. Some yeasts spoil food such as jam and fruit juices so food should be thrown out.

Viruses

These are very small micro-organisms, which multiply within living cells and not within the food itself. Viral food poisoning is often caught by a person touching an infected surface and then putting their fingers in their mouth. It can then be spread when the infected person handles food that is then eaten by someone else. Foods that have been linked to viral food poisoning include water, milk, salads and sandwiches.

✔ Chef's test

Choose the correct answer.

1. How can you tell if food has enough bacteria to cause food poisoning?
   a) It smells bad.
   b) It tastes bad.
   c) It looks bad.
   d) You can't tell. It looks, smells and tastes normal.

2. High-risk foods are foods that food poisoning bacteria grow well in. Which of these are high-risk foods?
   a) Dried, uncooked rice and pasta
   b) Flour and powdered, dry milk
   c) Fish, oysters and sushi
   d) Chocolate bars, boiled sweets

3. Low-risk foods are foods that bacteria don't grow well in. Which of these are low-risk foods?
   a) Eggs and egg products
   b) Raw and cooked meats
   c) Dried, uncooked rice and pasta
   d) Pizza and meat sandwiches

4. High-risk foods such as chicken should be cooked to an internal core temperature of:
   a) 60°C
   b) 75°C or higher
   c) 70°C
   d) 150°C

5. Which of the following may cause cross-contamination?
   a) Storing raw meat above cooked meat in a refrigerator.
   b) Drying your hands on a tea towel.
   c) Using a bacterial spray on work surfaces.
   d) Not washing your hands after handling raw chicken.

6. Explain the term 'cross-contamination'.

7. Give one example of
   a) Indirect contamination of food.
   b) Direct contamination of food.

🔍 Hint

To reinforce your knowledge of bacteria, watch the following video clips at http://www.bbc.co.uk/learningzone/clips/

209 Bacterial growth

2277 The Bacteria on our hands

2279 Understanding the size of bacteria

Countdown for

10 ... 9 ... 8 ... 7 ... 6 ... **5** ... 4 ... 3 ... 2 ... 1 ...

Wise up to the dangers

5: Watch your step

When working in the hospitality industry it is extremely important to spot areas of danger and put preventative measures in place to reduce the risk of accidents. No matter how big or small the kitchen, they all have dangers. The smaller the kitchen, the more compact the area is and this lack of space can lead to accidents. The larger the kitchen, the more staff are involved, and this brings another set of risks, such as sometimes staff leaving it to others to clean up spills.

The most common hazards in the hospitality industry

Hazard	Cause	Prevention
Slips, trips, falls	Slipping on a wet floor or tripping on uneven surfaces	• Mop up spills immediately and put out signs to warn others in the kitchen that the floor may still be slippy.
Cuts	Cutting equipment such as knives and electric meat slicers	• Hold the knife securely with your stronger hand. • Curl your fingers and cut away from them. • **Secure** the cutting board to a **flat** work surface and place a **damp cloth** under it to stop it slipping. • Use the **right size** of knife for the job and make sure it is **sharp**.
Burns/scalds	Hot surfaces, e.g. baking trays, plates, ovens. Hot liquids, e.g. water, fat, soup.	• **Open lids** away from you and always put pots of **boiling liquid** on the back rings of the cooker. • Use **dry oven cloths/gloves** when **handling hot** pans/dishes/trays. • **Don't overheat** oil as it can burst into flames. Never **leave oil to heat unattended.** • **Don't let pan handles stick out** over the edge of the cooker.
Strains/back injuries	Lifting and handling heavy or awkward-shaped objects.	• Always bend your knees when lifting heavy or awkward objects. • Get a second person to assist you. • Use a trolley system to move heavy objects.

The chance that the above hazards will result in an injury for young workers is higher when they are combined with risk factors, such as:

- lack of supervision
- inexperience
- trying to impress the boss, supervisor or co-workers

- temporary employment
- long working days.

When hazards are combined with risk factors they are called **dangerous combinations**.

First aid kit

A first aid kit must be placed in any hospitality kitchen and it must be maintained on a regular basis. There should also be a trained first aider on the staff.

✔ Chef's test

Complete the following:

1. List the items that should be in a first aid kit in a kitchen.
2. In groups, make up a wall display on how to prevent each of the four most common hazards in a hospitality kitchen.
3. Try out the virtual kitchen from the following website:

   http://www.safework.sa.gov.au/contentPages/EducationAndTraining/ActivitiesAndTests/VirtualKitchen/vkitchenframe.htm

Countdown for

10 ... 9 ... 8 ... 7 ... 6 ... 5 ... **4** ... 3 ... 2 ... 1 ...

4: Weighing and measuring

Whether you are a pupil cooking in school or a professional chef, measuring ingredients is of key importance. The correct balance of ingredients will not only ensure that food turns out looking and tasting great, but also that ratios of ingredients produce the proper consistency and texture. In school, recipes usually serve 2 or 4 portions.

The hospitality industry prepares food for much larger numbers of people, which would result in the following:

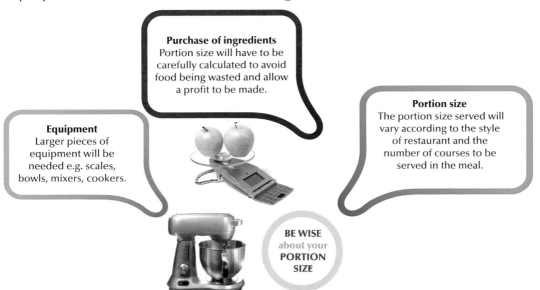

Purchase of ingredients
Portion size will have to be carefully calculated to avoid food being wasted and allow a profit to be made.

Portion size
The portion size served will vary according to the style of restaurant and the number of courses to be served in the meal.

Equipment
Larger pieces of equipment will be needed e.g. scales, bowls, mixers, cookers.

BE WISE about your **PORTION SIZE**

How to scale up a recipe

Ordering or requisitioning ingredients are an important part of a head chef's job. To work out the total ingredients to be ordered, the chef will have to 'scale up' recipes depending on the number of portions being made.

Scaling Up

The quantity of thickening and seasoning must be recalculated when scaling up as cooking times will be longer for larger quantities.

Hint: 'Taste as You Go' is good advice. Remember you can always add more seasoning but you can't take it out!

The quantity of ingredients in the original recipe can be multiplied once the number of portions required is known.

Not all ingredients need to be fully multiplied during scaling up, for example oil needed for sauteing, as long as there is enough to cover the bottom of the pan.

Hint: Care must also be taken with spices

✔ Chef's test

Complete the following:

1. Scale up the recipe for Chilli Con Carne from 2 to 4 portions.

Chilli Con Carne: 2 portions
100 g mince
50 g onion
100 ml tinned chopped tomatoes
15 ml tomato purée
75 g kidney beans
5 ml chilli powder
50 ml beef stock
75 g patna rice

2. You are preparing muffins as part of a coffee break for people at a conference. The following recipe will produce 12 blueberry muffins. Scale up the recipe to produce 6 dozen muffins. You may want to try this out.

Blueberry Muffins
110 g butter
250 g plain flour
250 g caster sugar
2 eggs
125 ml milk
10 ml baking powder
225 g fresh blueberries

Countdown for

10 ... 9 ... 8 ... 7 ... 6 ... 5 ... 4 ... **3** ... 2 ... 1 ...

3: Reading a recipe

Always read the recipe thoroughly before you start to cook. This will allow you to:

- see all the skills and techniques involved in the preparation of the recipe
- check how long food takes to cook
- consider how much time should be allocated to each step
- find out if chilling or resting time is needed.

Recipe formats

Recipes used in school, in magazines and recipe books may all be written differently. Some chefs will use handy measures but it is much more accurate to weigh and measure the ingredients.

All ingredients can be weighed and measured during preparation time and certain ingredients can have some preparation carried out in advance.

It is important that weighing and measuring is done accurately as your end results will be affected. Certain ingredients must be weighed after preparation.

When you are completing the practical assignment, the recipe will be written using the format on the following page.

Tuna Layer Bake (4 portions)

Ingredients

Courgette 75 g (prepared weight) ← *Prepared weight means you must weigh the ingredients after you have prepared them (grated).*

Garlic (peeled) 10 ml (prepared weight) ←
Onion (peeled) 100 g (prepared weight) *These ingredients can be prepared (peeled) before you start the assignment*

Sunflower oil 15 ml
Canned chopped tomatoes 400 ml (including liquid)
Passata 100 ml
Sugar 5 ml
Vegetable stock 100 ml
Green pepper 50 g (prepared weight) ← *Prepared weight: you must order a larger quantity of ingredient as some waste will be removed during preparation.*

White cheddar cheese 100 g
Green pesto 30 g
Canned sweetcorn 50 g (drained weight)
Canned tuna fish 150 g (drained weight) ← *These ingredients must have the liquid drained off before being weighed.*
Lasagne sheets 5–6
Seasoning

Method

Oven 200°C/Gas Mark 6 (where fan assisted ovens are used, the temperature should be adjusted accordingly)

1. Wash, dry and grate the courgette.
2. Finely chop the garlic.
3. Finely chop the onion.
4. Heat the oil in a large pan.
5. Add the garlic and onion, cover and sweat for 3 minutes. ← *In the method you are expected to use the skills you have gained, e.g. 'sweat' does not tell you how to do this, you are expected to know how to do it.*
6. Remove from the heat; add the courgette, chopped tomatoes, passata, sugar and the stock to the pan.
7. Bring to the boil; reduce the heat and simmer for 10 minutes.
8. Cut the green pepper into dice 5 × 5 × 5mm (macedoine). ← *You are expected to know the type of knife to use and how to cut the dice.*
9. Grate the cheese and reserve.
10. Remove the sauce from the heat, add the pesto, stir and taste for seasoning.
11. Adjust seasoning if required.
12. Spread a thin layer of the tomato sauce on the bottom of an ovenproof dish, 22 cm × 22 cm approximately.
13. Add the green pepper, sweetcorn and tuna fish to the remaining tomato sauce.
14. Place a layer of lasagne on top of the tomato sauce in the ovenproof dish.
15. Spread half of the tuna mixture evenly on top of the lasagne.
16. Cover with the remaining lasagne sheets.
17. Spread the remaining tuna mixture over the lasagne.
18. Cover with the grated cheese and bake for 30–35 minutes. ← *When you put the dish in the oven make sure you take a note of the time.*
19. Clean the dish and serve hot, garnished appropriately.

Skills	Timings
• Vegetable preparation • Sweating • Simmering • Baking	Check the timings carefully. • Sweating 3 minutes • Simmering 10 minutes • Baking 30–35 minutes • Remember to allow for serving times.

Countdown for

10 ... 9 ... 8 ... 7 ... 6 ... 5 ... 4 ... 3 ... **2** ... 1 ...

2: Document your progress

The teacher's role	Your role
To let you know: • When you are carrying out the assessments. • What you need to do to achieve the assessment. • The evidence and checklists you need to complete. • How and where to keep your evidence safe. Your teacher will complete observational checklists on your progress and give you feedback.	• Record your progress each time you are assessed. • Make sure you **name** and **date** each piece of evidence. • Keep your work in a safe place as this will be needed as evidence to show you have achieved each of the units.

⊘ Hint

Evidence may take the form of a workbook or a portfolio of each piece of evidence.

⊘ Hint

If you have been absent and had to complete your assessment on a different day it is important that you keep your records up-to-date.

Below is a sample recording sheet you might be given to record your progress at National 5 level.

Cookery Skills, Techniques and Processes (National 5) Unit: Candidate checklist

Name:

Dish	1.1 Weigh and measure			1.2 Food preparation techniques																																	Date achieved
	Scales	Jug	Measuring spoon	Peel/skin	Chop	Slice	Julienne	Brunoise	Jardiniere	Macedoine	Paysanne	Chiffonade	Segment	Blanche	Concasse	Puree	Marinate	Strain	Pass	Grate	Coat	Pane	Mix	Blend	Whisk	Cream	Fold	Rub in	Knead	Roll out	Portion	Shape	Line	Bake blind	Glaze	Pipe	
Beef Lasagne	✓	✓	✓	✓	✓	✓				✓										✓																	19/6/ 2014
Apple Meringue Pie	✓	✓	✓	✓		✓																			✓		✓	✓	✓	✓			✓	✓		✓	21/6/ 2014

Hint

Remember that some of your evidence could be used as part of your e-portfolio.

Below is a sample recording sheet you might be given to record your progress at National 4 level.

Cookery Skills, Techniques and Processes (National 4) Candidate checklist

Name:

Dish	1.1 Weigh and measure			1.2 Food preparation techniques															2.1 Cooking ingredients 2.2 Controlling cookery processes and testing for readiness						2.3	1.3 2.4	Date achieved
	Scales	Measuring jug	Measuring spoons	Peel	Chop	Slice	Dice	Grate	Marinate	Puree	Blend	Mix	Whisk	Cream	Fold	Rub in	Knead	Shape	Roll out	Glaze	Steam	Boil	Bake	Grill	Stew	Stir fry	Garnish/decorate	Safety and hygiene	
Spaghetti Bolognese	✓	✓	✓	✓	✓	✓	✓															✓			✓		✓	✓	02/04/ 2014
Apple and Blackberry Crumble	✓		✓			✓						✓				✓							✓				✓		01/05/ 2014

Countdown for

10 ... 9 ... 8 ... 7 ... 6 ... 5 ... 4 ... 3 ... 2 ... **1** ...

1: Never a problem, only a solution

Sometimes things don't work out as you planned in the kitchen. So what do you do?

1. Don't panic.
2. Try to solve the problem.

Sauces/stews/soups

Problem	Solution
The sauce/stew/ soup is too thin.	• Simmer it with the lid off. • Thicken with the appropriate thickening agent (e.g. cornflour, arrowroot).
The sauce/stew/ soup is too thick.	• Add a little more liquid such as water, stock or milk.
The sauce has gone lumpy.	• Sieve the sauce. • Blend then pass through a fine sieve. • Start again if too lumpy.
The sauce/stew/ soup lacks flavour.	• Lack of flavour – add seasoning or a further flavouring, e.g. sherry vinegar, lemon juice, cream or concentrated stock.
The sauce/stew/ soup is too salty	• Add some more liquid.

🔍 **Hint**

When making a cheese sauce, bring the sauce to the boil first then take the **pan off the heat** before adding the cheese – this will stop the cheese from separating (there will be enough heat in the sauce to melt the cheese).

🔍 **Hint**

You may need to thicken the sauce/stew/soup with a little cornflour blended with cold water to achieve the correct consistency.

Baking/grilling

Problem – Cakes	Solution
The cake mixture is starting to curdle	• Beat in a little of the sieved flour to stop it curdling.
Cake sinks in the middle	• During baking: don't open oven too early. • After it has been removed from the oven, disguise the dip in the middle by decorating it carefully.
Cake sticks to inside of tin	• Before turning into the tin make sure it is greased and lined properly. • Follow the baking time on the recipe. • Run a knife around the inside edge of the tin to release it but make sure you don't rip the edge of the cake.
The cake has not risen well	**Before baking make sure you:** • weigh ingredients correctly. • whisk the eggs and sugar until they leave a trail on the surface. You should be able to either draw a figure 8 or your initials on the top and it will stay there. • Do not over fold or whisk in the flour. **After it has been baked:** • Decorate it to disguise it or start again.
Top of cake not browning quickly enough	• Have patience — allow it to bake at the temperature set. • Turn the oven up slightly if you know it is cooked through and you only need it to brown otherwise you could end up with a brown crust and a raw sponge inside.
Top of cake browning too quickly, sponge not cooked	• Turn the oven down.

Problem – Meringues	Solution
Egg white is over-whipped and starting to separate	• Throw it out and start again as the mixture will not hold its shape when piped.
Egg whites won't whisk up	Before starting, make sure: • there is no egg yolk in the bowl • the bowl is clean and dry.
Whisked egg white is losing its shape	• Always add the sugar gradually and don't over fold it in.

🔍 **Hint**

Crumble meringue and use as a topping if it has cracked or lost shape.

🔍 **Hint**

Watch the short clip on how to line a pastry case: http://www.ifood.tv/video/how-to-line-a-flan-case-with-pastry.

Problem – Browning of dishes	Solution
Dishes browning at one side	• Turn the item round in the oven so that the other side browns.
Stop a dish browning too quickly	• Turn the oven/grill down. • If the dish is in the oven, lightly cover the top of it with tin foil, e.g. shepherds' pie. NB: Cheese will stick to the tin foil.
Grated cheese/crumb toppings not browning quickly enough	• Place under a hot grill to brown or turn the oven up.

Problem – Pastry making	Solution
Pastry over-rubbed in and greasy	• Throw it out and start again. • If your hands are too hot, cool them by running your wrists under cold water – this will cool the blood flowing into your hands/fingers.
Pastry dough too hard to roll	• Bring back to room temperature if it has been in a fridge.
Flan ring lined with pastry has a crack or hole in it or the sides are too short	**Before baking:** • dampen the pastry (with water) round the area needing repair and seal with a piece of pastry. Flatten into shape. **After baking:** • If there is a hole in the pastry after baking, plug with a little left-over pastry (only if the hole is not too big and the flan case is to be cooked further). • Small cracks – brush with a little egg to seal it. • Keep any left over pastry in the fridge to use for patching any small holes if the pastry has to be returned to the oven for further cooking.
Shrinkage	• Make sure you push pastry down into the corners to stop it shrinking back too much. • Allow to rest before trimming.

Using the hob

Problem	Solution
Melted fat sparking or beginning to smoke	• Remove from the heat, e.g. slide carefully onto an unused area of the hob and allow to cool slightly before using. • Do not add any water into the pan. • Make sure food to be cooked is as dry as possible, e.g. vegetables and meat.
Fat on fire in the pan	• Do not move the pan. • Turn off the heat and cover with a fire blanket or a baking tray to exclude the air. • Leave to cool before moving.
Sauteeing, e.g. onions, mushrooms, peppers	• If it starts to brown, take off heat, add a splash of COLD oil to cool the pan and stir to prevent bits burning.

Pasta/rice

🔍 Hint

Pasta should be served 'al dente'. Al dente is a term used to describe pasta that's fully cooked, but not overly soft. The phrase is Italian for 'to the tooth,' or 'to the bite' which comes from testing the pasta's consistency with your teeth.

Problem	Solution
Rice turning sticky	Before cooking: • Place rice in a sieve and rinse thoroughly with cold water to remove the starch. After cooking: • Pour into a sieve and rinse with boiling water.
Pasta over-cooking	• Pour into a sieve, rinse with boiling water then stir in a little olive oil.
Risotto sticking to the pan before rice is cooked	• Stir in a little more liquid (stock/water) and allow to reduce before serving.

Whipping cream

Problem	Solution
Over-whipped and about to separate	• Throw it out and start again if it has started to turn to butter. • Stir in a little more cold cream or whole milk if it is just starting to go beyond piping consistency – do not beat the mixture.

✔ Chef's test

Complete the following:

1. Your hands are too hot and your pastry has become over-rubbed in and gone sticky. What can you do?

2. You are making Macaroni Cheese but are having a bad day! Explain what actions need to be taken to solve the following problems.
   a) The pasta is starting to over cook.
   b) The cheese sauce is too thick.
   c) The top of the dish is not browning well and you are running out of time.

3. You have slightly over-whipped your cream. Describe what to do to stop it separating.

4. You have just taken your flan case for a quiche out of the oven and discovered there is a hole in it. Explain what can you do to remedy the problem.

Unit 1 Cookery Skill, Techniques and Processes

What's this unit all about?

This unit will develop your knowledge and understanding of the range of cookery skills, food preparation techniques and cookery processes.

This knowledge will be applied during practical cookery.

You will also develop an understanding of the importance of safe and hygienic practices during the production of dishes.

By the end of this unit you should be able to:

Outcome 1: Use cookery skills to prepare ingredients

This means you have to:

- Select and use equipment to weigh and measure ingredients accurately
- Apply a range of food preparation techniques using appropriate equipment with precision
- Work safely and hygienically

Outcome 2: Follow cookery processes to produce dishes :

This means you have to:

- Cook prepared ingredients according to recipes
- Control the stages of the cookery processes and test food for readiness
- Present and garnish or decorate the dishes and, where appropriate, portion them
- Work safely and hygienically

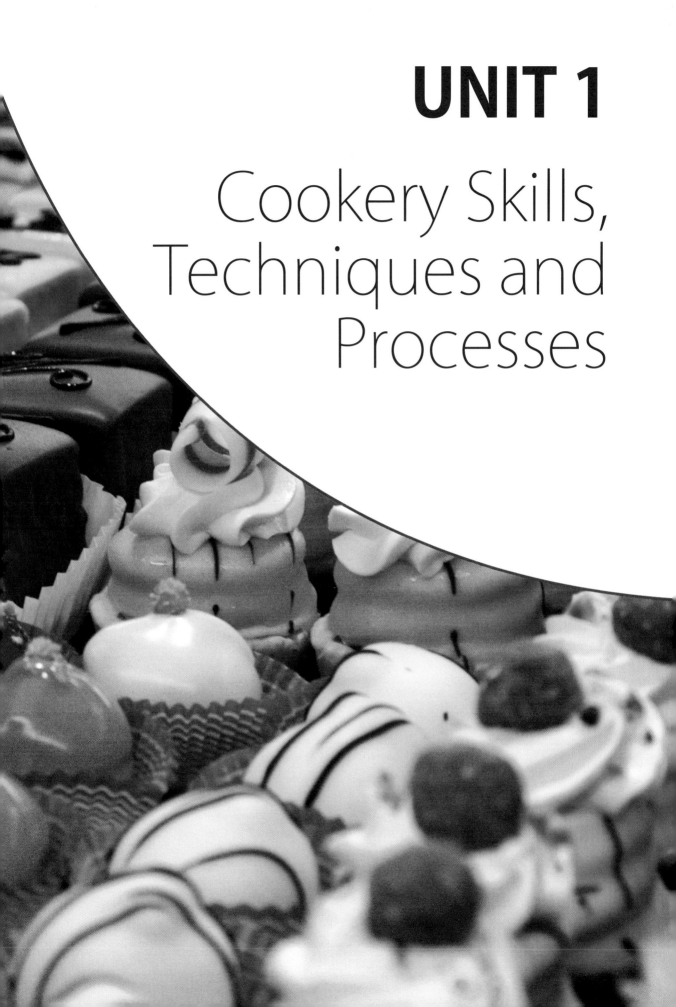

UNIT 1

Cookery Skills, Techniques and Processes

1 Tools and you

By the end of this chapter you should be able to:

- Select and use equipment to weigh and measure ingredients accurately.
- Apply a range of food preparation techniques using appropriate equipment with precision.
- Work safely and hygienically.

Topic 1: Cut it

This section looks at the basic equipment you will need when working in a range of sections in a hospitality kitchen.

Common kitchen knives

There are many pieces of equipment available for chefs to use when preparing food, however, the most essential piece of equipment is a proper set of knives and a steel for sharpening them.

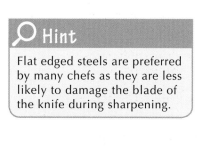

Hint

Flat edged steels are preferred by many chefs as they are less likely to damage the blade of the knife during sharpening.

Cleaver   Bread   Boning   Chef's   Carving   Vegetable

Although chefs have many different knives, there are two knives that they use on a daily basis.

- **Vegetable knife:** A vegetable knife is a small knife with a plain edge blade that is ideal for peeling and other small or tricky work (such as de-veining a shrimp, removing the seeds from a chilli, cutting small garnishes). It is designed to be an all-purpose knife, similar to a chef's knife, except smaller. Vegetable knives are usually between 6 and 10 cm long.
- **Chef's knife:** this is an all-purpose knife that is curved to allow the chef to rock the knife on the cutting board for a more precise cut. Chef's knives are usually 15–30 cm in length, with 20 cm the most common size.

Hint

In the hospitality industry, a vegetable knife is often referred to as a paring knife.

? Did you know

A chef's knife is also known as a cook's knife or French knife.

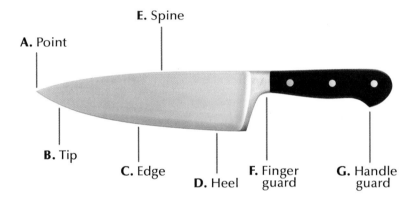

E. Spine

A. Point

B. Tip

C. Edge

D. Heel

F. Finger guard

G. Handle guard

A	Point	The very end of the knife, which is used for piercing.
B	Tip	The first third of the blade (approximately) is used for small or delicate work because it is curved.
C	Edge	The entire cutting surface of the knife, which extends from the point to the heel. The edge may be bevelled or symmetric.
D	Heel	The rear part of the blade, used for cutting activities that require more force.
E	Spine	The top, thicker portion of the blade, which adds weight and strength.
F	Handle guard	The lip below the end of the handle, which gives the knife a better grip and prevents slipping.
G	Finger guard	The part that keeps the chef's hand from slipping onto the blade.

How to use a chef's knife properly

The technique for using a chef's knife is an individual preference, however, most cooks prefer to grip the handle, with all four fingers and the thumb gathered underneath.

For fine slicing, the handle is raised up and down while the tip remains in contact with the cutting board and the cut object is pushed under the blade.

Techniques include chop, slice, julienne, brunoise, jardinière, macedoine, paysanne, chiffonade, segment and concassé.

Other knives

- A palette knife is not a sharp knife, but is very useful for coating and shaping foods.

- A vegetable peeler is also a very important piece of equipment.

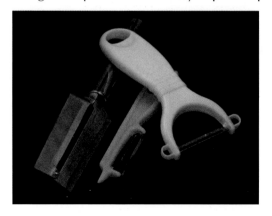

? Did you know?

In an industrial kitchen, there may be large-scale cutting equipment such as food processors and peelers to help make the task of preparing large quantities of foods much quicker and easier. However, it is important to remember that small pieces of equipment, such as graters, are also required.

🔍 Hint

There are other styles of vegetable peelers, e.g. Y peelers.

Other pieces of equipment used for cutting

- **Food processors** have different blades and attachments for chopping, grating and slicing. They can also be used for other processes such as blending, puréeing and dough making.
- **Hand blenders** can be used for puréeing/blending soups, or for making a small amount of breadcrumbs. Some hand blenders are designed so the blade section can be separated from the main unit.

> **Hint**
>
> Care should be taken when cleaning either of these pieces of equipment. They must be switched off before disassembling and remember the blades are extremely sharp.

It is all in the colour

Cross-contamination is one of the most common causes of food-related illnesses such as **food poisoning**. This is when harmful bacteria transfer from one food product to another by way of contaminated tools, equipment or hands. It is therefore very important to make sure knives are thoroughly washed and dried at the end of every task.

In many cases of cross-contamination however, **chopping boards** are the prime culprit. For that reason, using separate, **colour-coded** chopping boards for different ingredients is a great way of preventing cross-contamination.

Here are the different cutting board colours and what they should be used for.

> **Hint**
>
> Place a damp netcloth or paper towel under the chopping board to prevent it moving while preparing food.

A **metal storage rack** allows the air to circulate around the chopping boards, preventing any moulds developing.

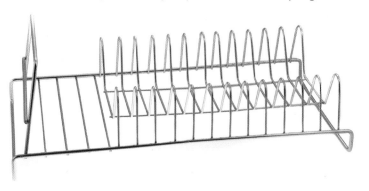

✔ Chef's test

Complete the following:

1. Which two knives are the most commonly used by chefs?
2. Watch the training video 'Basic Knife Skills by Josh Rockman.
3. What type of steel is preferred **by chefs** for sharpening knives? Using the Internet, find out about the range of large-scale cutting equipment available for use in a large-scale kitchen.
4. You have been asked to prepare a beef and vegetable stir fry – which **colour** chopping boards will you need?

🔍 Hint

To 'prepare' vegetables, means to take off the outer skin and remove any seeds.

All the vegetables should be a similar size when cut up so they cook evenly.

You can use other flavoured oils, or add a sauce to the prepared vegetables.

🍳 Service chef!

1. Use a paring knife and vegetable peeler to prepare a selection of vegetables.
2. Trial out the technique for using a cook's knife to cut up the prepared vegetables for a stir fry. (refer to Chapter 2 for advice on getting the techniques right).
3. Stir fry your prepared vegetables in a little garlic-infused oil then add a dash of soy sauce at the end. Season to taste.

🔍 Hint

Always make sure scales are set at zero before weighing, measuring jugs are placed on a flat, level surface and measuring spoons are levelled off.

Topic 2: Bake it

This section looks at the basic food preparation equipment you will need when working in the pastry section of a kitchen. Remember that these pieces of equipment may also be used in other kitchen sections.

Weighing and measuring

Weighing and measuring is important to successful baking and cooking, therefore it is essential to weigh and measure ingredients accurately. A set of scales, measuring spoons and different sizes of measuring jugs are the basic equipment required for this.

Cooling tray

A tray made from a network of stainless steel wires. The holes allow air to circulate around the food, cooling it down quickly and preventing it from becoming soggy. Hot cooked food is placed either directly onto the cooling tray to cool down or sometimes the food is left in the baking tray/tin to cool down first before turning out onto the cooling tray.

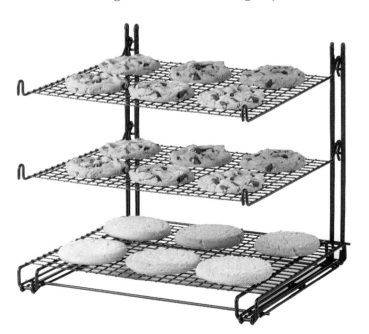

? Did you know?

There are different types of scales, manual and digital. Manual scales are useful for weighing large amounts of ingredients, and digital scales are good for very small, precise quantities of ingredients because they are available with a 1 g scale.

🔍 Hint

It is possible to purchase a tiered cooling tray rack, which allows more food to be cooled without taking up valuable space. This is particularly useful if the kitchen does not have a lot of spare work surface space.

Flour dredger

A container that has a tight fitting lid with small holes in it. It is used for sprinkling a light layer of flour onto a work surface when working with a dough (pastry/biscuit/bread/pizza).

Grater

A grater is a tool that grates and shreds food finely. Several types of graters feature different sizes of grating slots. They are commonly used to grate soft foods such as cheese, lemon or orange peel (zest). They can also be used to grate chocolate for decoration and harder ingredients such as nutmeg.

Box grater

Microplane grater

Mouli grater

Nutmeg grater

Rolling pin

A long cylindrical food preparation utensil that comes in two styles: rollers, which consist of a thick cylindrical roller with small handles at each end; and rod rolling pins, which are usually thin tapered batons. They are mainly used to shape and flatten dough but they can also be used for crushing biscuits and nuts.

Sieve

A kitchen tool made from different materials, such as stainless steel and nylon. The mesh dome comes in different sizes from medium to superfine. The finer the mesh, the finer the end result, e.g. the superfine mesh is good for dusting icing sugar and cocoa onto baked goods. Some sieves also have hooks that allow them to sit on top of bowls, and they may also have heat-resistant handles. Sieves are used to break up clumps of dry ingredients such as flour, as well as adding air and combining ingredients. They are also used to strain liquid, such as juice from tinned fruit.

Whisk

A whisk is a cooking utensil used in food preparation to blend ingredients to make them smooth, or to incorporate air into a mixture, in a process known as whisking or whipping. Most whisks consist of a long, narrow handle with a series of wire loops joined at the end. The wires are usually metal, but some are plastic for use with non-stick cookware. Electric hand-held whisks are also available. Whisks are commonly used to whip egg whites into a firm foam to make meringue, or to whisk eggs and sugar to make a fatless sponge. They are also useful for whipping cream for fillings and decoration. Whisks have differently-shaped loops depending on their intended functions:

Balloon whisk

- The most common shape is that of a wide teardrop, termed a 'balloon whisk'. Balloon whisks are best suited to mixing in bowls, as their curved edges conform to a bowl's concave sides.
- A flat whisk, sometimes referred to as a roux whisk, has the loops arranged in a flat successive pattern. It is useful for working in shallow-sided pans and bowls.

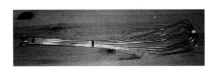

Flat whisk

41

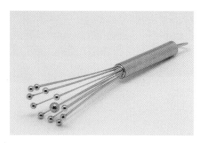

Ball whisk

- Ball whisks have no loops. Instead, a group of individual wires comes out of the handle, each tipped with a metal ball making it good for reaching into the corners of straight-sided pans. This whisk is easier to clean than traditional looped varieties.

- Hand-held electric whisks or mixers have a pair of rotating beaters and they have a range of speeds. They are useful for making whisked sponges, creamed mixtures and meringues as they are quicker and less tiring to use.

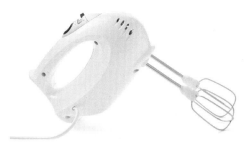

- In a large-scale kitchen you will find industrial mixers, which are useful for making up large batches of things like cake mixture.

Cookware

There are many different types of baking tins. The size and shape required depends upon the task to be carried out.

- **Baking trays/baking sheets** are flat, rectangular metal pans used in an oven. They are often used for baking bread rolls, pastries and flat products such as biscuits and Swiss rolls. They can be made from a variety of materials such as aluminium and stainless steel. Non-stick versions have been developed and come with additional features, such as a lip to prevent food sliding off them and handles to help when putting them in and taking them out of the oven.

- **Sandwich/cake tins**. Sandwich tins are used to make layered/sandwich cakes. These tins are used to make cakes that you sandwich together, for example a Victoria sandwich cake. These tins are shallower than other cake tins and are often used in pairs. Cake tins are used to make baked items that come in a variety of shapes and sizes. Cake tins may be round, square, rectangular or novelty

shaped. Some deeper cake tins have loose bottoms to make it easier to get the cake out once baked.

- **Muffin and patty tins**. These are a rectangular metal baking pan with six or twelve cups, used to bake both muffins and cupcakes. Muffin tin sizes are typically mini, standard and jumbo sized. Each cup is normally lined with paper baking cups, and then filled with muffin or cake batter. Patty tins are similar to muffin tins, but are shallower and used for individual tarts and sponge cakes. Both types are traditionally made of metal; most commonly aluminium, however, flexible silicone is now becoming more popular.

- **Silicone bakeware** ensures even baking and quick cooling and, thanks to its amazing non-stick properties, cakes simply pop out once baked. Silicone is easy to clean and it is easy to store as it springs back into shape instantly even if it has been rolled, folded or squashed.

Hint

Silicone bakeware is freezer and oven safe, up to a certain temperature.

- **Flan rings**. A flan ring is a metal ring with no bottom. The ring is set on a non-stick baking sheet, then filled. The baking sheet serves as the bottom of the pan. Flan rings are used to shape open-faced tarts, pastry shells, savoury flans and cheesecakes.

Hint

Flan rings may be either plain or fluted. Traditionally plain flan rings are used for savoury dishes and fluted for sweet flans.

? Did you know?

A cookie cutter is the American term for a biscuit cutter.

- **Biscuit cutters**, either plain or fluted, will help produce high-rising biscuits because the biscuit cutter has a sharp edge to produce a clean cut (cutters with a dull edge will compact the dough and the biscuits will not rise as well when baking). Round biscuit cutters are normally made of tin or stainless steel and come in a range of sizes. Biscuit cutters also come in a variety of shapes and sizes and can be linked to a theme such as chirstmas.

? Did you know?

A biscuit cutter can also double as a cookie and scone cutter or can be used to cut small cake rounds for individual servings or petit fours.

Other tools that are useful in this section of the kitchen are:

- **Spatula**: made of plastic or silicone and can be used for mixing and scraping out a mixture from a bowl.

- **Pastry brush**: a small brush used for glazing foods before or after cooking. It can also be used for greasing baking tins.

🔍 Hint

The most common pastry brushes are available with nylon bristles, however, you can get other types such as ones made from silicone.

- **Tablespoon/teaspoon**: both made from metal. A tablespoon is used for mixing ingredients together and folding in ingredients, e.g. for whisked sponges and meringues. A teaspoon is used for more precise work, such as garnishing/decorating plates and for tasting.

✔ Chef's test

Complete the following:

1. Which piece of equipment would a chef use to whip cream? Explain your answer.
2. Give a description of each of the three hand whisks.
3. What is a chinois and what is it used for?

♕ Service chef!

1. Prepare a batch of apple and cinnamon scones to show the use of a sieve, grater, baking tray and cooling tray.
2. Make a batch of muffins and bake them in a silicone muffin tin without any paper cases and test how easy they are to take out of the tin.
3. Use an electric whisk to make an all-in-one chocolate sponge and buttercream filling.

Topic 3: Cook it

This section looks at the equipment you will need when working in the meat and fish sections of a kitchen. Remember that these pieces of equipment may also be used in other kitchen sections. Having the right cookware is absolutely essential for the success of any restaurant. Without the right cookware for the job, the chefs are set up for failure.

Cost, ease of maintenance, metal type and shape are all important considerations when shopping for commercial cookware. The type of metal will determine the weight of the pan, its heat retention and whether it is corrosion and rust-proof. The most important thing is to choose a pot or pan that your chef and kitchen workers know how to work with.

Cookware includes everything from frying pans, sauce pans, sauté pans, pots and crêpe pans.

> ## 🔍 Hint
>
> Aluminium cookware products can withstand higher heat levels as well as the wear and tear of a professional kitchen. Cast iron cookware is also valued as it can also withstand and retain high heat levels.

When deciding on which pot/pan to purchase the following factors should also be considered:

Oven safe
The design and construction of the handles are important to ensure that they do not get too hot while in use.

Non-stick
This type of finish is beneficial for some tasks such as omelette making. Care must be taken, however, as the finish can be easily damaged.

Easy to clean
If not non-stick, the pans need to be easy for the staff to clean to save time.

Compatiblity
Can they be used with all types of cookers including induction hobs?

Even heat distribution
The base should give even heat distribution to prevent any 'hot spots'.

As well as pots and pans other items are also required in this section, such as:

- **Colander**: a bowl-shaped kitchen utensil with holes in it used for draining food such as pasta or rice. They are made of a light metal, such as aluminium or thinly rolled stainless steel.

- **Fish slice**: a kitchen tool with a wide flat blade and long holes. Used for lifting and turning food while cooking to prevent it breaking up.

- **Wooden spoons**. What to look for when selecting the right wooden spoon:

– **Stirring** is a spoon's primary task. It must have a wide surface area so that a significant amount of food can be moved around the pot with limited effort.

– **Scraping** is necessary to get cooking food off the bottom of the pot or for deglazing the browned bits off the bottom of the pan when making a sauce. A good spoon should be able to do this efficiently and effectively.

– **Heat-resistance** is important as a good flat edged should not melt if it rests on the side of a pan or is used to stir something that is boiling. It also allows the person using the spoon to do so without the use of oven gloves.

✅ Chef's test

Complete the following:

1. Give four points a chef should consider when purchasing pots and pans for a kitchen. Explain your answers.
2. Make up an advice sheet about the equipment required for the meat and fish sections of a restaurant.
3. List the benefits of non-stick pans and bakeware.

👨‍🍳 Service chef!

1. a) Select the cooking equipment required for making a pan of puréed lentil soup.
   b) Prepare and cook the soup.
   c) Evaluate the suitability of each of the following pieces of equipment used: knives, pan, blender.
2. Make an omelette in a non-stick pan and evaluate the end result.

Melon baller

🔍 Hint

Watch the video on You Tube on how to use a melon baller: *www.youtube.com/watch?v=cY8QmTJdm-Q*

❓ Did you know?

A melon baller is formally called a Parisienne scoop.

Zester

Julienne peeler

🔍 Hint

Watch the video on You Tube on how to use a julienne peeler *www.youtube.com/watch?v=3bNy8gxPFPo*

Topic 4: Serve it – all in the finish

This section looks at the equipment you might come across when working in the garnish section of a kitchen. Remember that these pieces of equipment may also be found in other sections of the kitchen.

The way a dish is presented is extremely important to the customer. Where a dish is appealing to the eye, it is more appealing to the palate.

Small cutting equipment for presentation

- **Melon baller:** a small spoon-like tool used to cut round or oval-shaped sections of melon by pressing them into the melon's flesh and rotating it. It can also be used to cut other soft fruit and vegetables, such as potatoes known as "pomme de terre". They are available in a variety of sizes and some have the handle in the middle and a different-sized bowl on each end. The bowl has a small hole in the middle to allow air and juice through, making it easier to remove the food.

- **Zester:** used for getting the zest from lemons and other citrus fruit. It has a curved metal end, the top of which is perforated with a row of round holes with sharpened rims. To use a zester you must press the metal end against the fruit and draw it across the peel. The sharp rims cut the zest from the pith underneath. Chefs also use the 'microplane' grater to remove the zest from the fruit (see page 40)

- **Julienne peeler:** used to cut vegetables into long, thin, even-sized strips. It works in a similar way to a potato peeler but the blades are specially shaped to give 'julienne' strips.

- **Small cutters:** many cutters are now available in different shapes and sizes. They can be used to cut out shapes from fruit and vegetables but they are also very good for cutting out chocolate shapes.

- **Butter curler:** some hospitality establishments use a butter curler to shape butter into delicate butter curls. This is a good way of portioning butter.

Piping bags and nozzles

A **piping bag** is a cone-shaped bag that can be filled with cream, dough or creamed potato. It can be used for all sorts of dishes, from rounds of choux pastry to perfect meringues or potato croquettes, as well as cream for decorating a dish. They are made from materials such as polyester and nylon, which can be washed and re-used. Disposable piping bags can be purchased which are more hygienic and save time for the chef. Here are some instructions on how to fill a piping bag:

1. Place the right size and shape of nozzle into the small end of the bag. Make sure the seam side of the bag is on the outside.

2. Pull the large end of the bag over your hand.

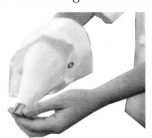

3. Spoon some of the mixture into the bag, pulling it from the spoon using your covered hand.

4. When the bag is full enough, squeeze the mixture towards the nozzle to remove any air pockets.

5. Twist the remaining fabric at the other end of the bag around the mixture.

6. Pipe the mixture by squeezing with only one hand and using your other hand to support the nozzle-end of the bag.

7. Hold the piping bag just above the nozzle.

8. Squeeze the mixture onto the cake you are decorating or baking tray if profiteroles, moving the bag in a small circle. Stop squeezing before you lift the nozzle away. Press down lightly and pull the piping bag up sharply.

If you are doing chocolate run-outs or more intricate piping it may be necessary to make a small piping bag out of grease-proof paper:

1. Cut a 250 mm square out of grease-proof paper. Fold in half to make a triangle. Use a smaller size for less icing.

2. Working with the long side facing away from you, pull one corner into the centre.

3. Hold in place while bending in the other corner and wrapping tightly to form a cone shape.

4. Tuck upstanding ends inside the paper cone and fold down to secure. Spoon the melted chocolate into the bag. Fold down the bag to seal. Snip off the tip gently and apply pressure to pipe out contents. Practice will make you perfect.

Hint

Watch http://www.bbc.co.uk/food/techniques/using_piping_bags to find out how to fill and use a piping bag.

Step 1

Step 2

Step 3

Step 4

The most common **piping nozzles** are plain and star-shaped and are available in a variety of sizes.

- **Plain nozzles**: small nozzles are used for fine and decorative work and larger ones can be used for piping potatoes or dough such as choux pastry for eclairs.

- **Star nozzles**: small nozzles are used for fine and decorative work and larger ones can be used for piping potatoes, dough, cream or meringue.

Hint

As part of your course you are more likely to use the larger nozzles.

☑ Chef's test

Complete the following:

1. Use the instructions given to make a paper piping bag.

2. What would a grease-proof paper piping bag be used for?

3. Give three examples of foods that might be piped using a large nozzle.

👨‍🍳 Service chef!

1. Using the paper piping bag you made, fill it with a little melted chocolate and pipe some chocolate run-outs onto parchment paper.

2. Make a mandarin gateau and decorate the top with piped cream, mandarins and your chocolate run-outs to show four even portions.

3. Make up a batch of profiteroles or chocolate eclairs, fill with whipped cream and coat with chocolate sauce.

🔵 End of chapter activities

Activity 1

As a class

Arrange a visit to the school canteen or a hotel in your area. Make a list of all the large-scale equipment used in the kitchen.

Working on your own

Use available resources to investigate the range of large-scale equipment you have listed. For each piece of equipment find out the following information:

a) use

b) how to use it safely

c) cleaning required

d) cost

Activity 2

Working on your own

Make up a booklet called *The A–Z Guide to Equipment*, which could be used in a hospitality kitchen. You can either list the names or find pictures of the equipment.

Activity 3

Group task

1. Half the group should make a jam Swiss roll using a balloon whisk and the other half should make the same recipe using an electric hand-held whisk.

2. Carry out a comparison of the two pieces of equipment using the following headings:
   - Ease of preparation
   - Finished product

Activity 4

Working in pairs

Develop a game to help a first year catering student match equipment with its use. It could be: dominoes, bingo, trumps, millionaire or could be a wordsearch or crossword. Trial your game with others in the class.

Rate Your Progress

How confident are you that you have achieved each of the following objectives?

Using the following key as a guide, give yourself a rating for each of the objectives below.

Rating	Explanation
1	Confident with the standard of my work.
2	Fairly confident with the standard of my work.
3	The majority of my work was satisfactory.
4	Require to do some further work.
5	Require a lot of work.

Objectives	Rating
Select and use equipment to weigh and measure ingredients accurately.	
Apply a range of food preparation techniques using appropriate equipment with precision.	
Work safely and hygienically.	

Looking at your ratings

Write down two next steps to 'unlocking' your knowledge of cookery skills, techniques and processes.

2 Cookery skills, techniques and processes

By the end of this chapter you should be able to:

- Select and use equipment to weigh and measure ingredients accurately.
- Apply a range of food preparation techniques using appropriate equipment with precision.
- Cook prepared ingredients according to recipes.
- Control the stages of the cookery processes and testing food for readiness.
- Present and garnish or decorate the dishes and, where appropriate, portion them.
- Work safely and hygienically.

Topic 1: Food preparation techniques

Many techniques are very basic and used frequently, such as peel, grate, slice and chop, however, there are many other more complicated techniques that require to be mastered in the hospitality industry such as:

Cut to size

Different techniques used in the preparation of fruit and vegetables are shown opposite.

Cuts such as the dice, may be used as part of a dish, however the baton and matchstick size of cuts are more likely to be used for a stir fry recipe.

> **🔍 Hint**
>
> Instructions in recipes will give you the size and shape of cut required.

The most important thing to remember when preparing any of the above cuts is to make sure that all the pieces are the same size when prepared. This will help to ensure even cooking.

The following cuts may be used for garnishing a plate:

- **Chiffonade:** lettuce and other fine leaves are cut into even shreds or strips.
- **Concassé:** a food e.g. tomato is skinned then the flesh is finely chopped.
- **Segment:** the process of removing the skin of fruits, then dividing the flesh into natural wedges e.g. orange.

Cutting Techniques

Matchstick size
1mm thick x 20mm long, known as **julienne** strips.

Very small dice
2mm x 2mm x 2mm for use in recipes. known as **brunoise.**

Small cubed dice
3mm x 3mm x 3mm
(or 5mm x 5mm x 5mm)
known as **macedoine.**

Batons
5mm x 5mm x 15mm sometimes
3mm x 3mm x 18mm
known as **jardinière.**

Thin flat triangles, squares or rounds
1cm sided triangles or squares or 1 cm diameter rounds.
known as **paysanne.**

Blanche

Coat

The ABC of techniques used in the preparation of a range of ingredients

- **Blanche:** Food is immersed into boiling water then plunged into ice-cold water ('refreshed') to stop the cooking process, e.g. to loosen tomato skins before skinning or to preserve colour in green vegetables before freezing.

- **Coat:** To cover a food with a batter, sauce or other protective coating, e.g. breadcrumbs for fishcakes or Scotch eggs. This is used to protect the food during the cooking process.

- **Marinate:** Foods are covered in a liquid or paste for a controlled length of time, e.g. red meat could be marinated in red wine, chicken in a spicy marinade. This helps to make the food more tender after cooking and it adds flavour.

- **Mix and blend:**
  Mixing combines ingredients evenly with a spoon or mixer, e.g. mixing coleslaw ingredients together.
  Blend combines two or more ingredients together to form a paste, usually a starchy powder with a liquid, e.g. cornflour and water to thicken a sauce.

- **Portion:** the amount of a particular food that is served to one person.
- **Purée:** to grind or mash food until it forms a smooth, thick mixture, e.g. soups or vegetable purées to be serve with meat, poultry or fish. This can be done through a sieve, blender or food processor.

Purée

- **Strain and pass:** Straining is where liquid is separated from solid through a strainer, e.g. a colander can be used for vegetables or pasta. Passing is where a liquid or purée is put through a fine mesh sieve or strainer to make it smooth and lump-free, e.g. fruit coulis.

Strain

The ABC of techniques used in the preparation of a range of ingredients for baking

- **Bake blind:** the method of cooking a pastry flan case without the filling.
- **Cream:** to beat and mix an ingredient or a combination of ingredients to a smooth, creamy consistency e.g. caster sugar and margarine when making a Victoria sandwich cake.
- **Dough making:**
  - **Rub in:** the process of incorporating fat into flour until the mixture resembles fine breadcrumbs e.g. shortcrust pastry. This can be done by hand or food processor.

Cream

Rub in

- **Knead:** to work dough with your hands. Fold the dough back towards you, press forward with the palms/heel of your hands, turn the dough and repeat for as long as the recipe says e.g. pastry, scone, biscuit or bread.

Hint

If your fingertips are too hot run your wrists under cold water to cool down the blood flow into your fingertips.

Knead

Fold

Line

– Never over-handle pastry or scone dough, as this will make it tough. Always let pastry dough rest before baking to prevent it from shrinking. A lot of kneading is required in bread making to develop the dough and to prevent air bubbles in the finished product.

- **Fold:** to mix gently, bringing the spatula or the edge of a tablespoon down through the mixture, across the bottom, then back up over the top (in a figure of eight) until mixed. Little air is lost in this method, e.g. folding in sugar to a meringue mix or a whisked sponge mix.

- **Glaze:** to brush the surface with a substance to give the food a glossy finish e.g. glazing scones, pastry with an egg wash.

- **Line:** to cover the bottom and sides of a dish with pastry e.g. a flan or bacon if making a terrine.

- **Pipe:** to force a paste, icing, cream or stuffing or similar substance from a piping bag, e.g. decorating a gateau with cream, Viennese whirls, etc.

Pipe

- **Roll out:** to flatten and spread with a rolling pin, associated with pie crusts, cookies, or dough.

- **Shape:** the process of taking food ingredients, e.g. burger mix, pastry dough, fishcake mix and forming them into a particular shape. Shaping can be done in different ways by using:
  – hands or a palette knife when making burgers/fishcakes
  – a knife to cut food into a particular shape
  – pastry cutters to shape biscuits, scones and individual pastry cases.

- **Whisk:** the process of adding air to a mixture through the use of a hand or electric whisk, e.g. whisking egg whites for meringues.

Whisk

✔ Chef's test

Complete the following:
1. Describe the difference between mix and blend.
2. Describe the difference between brunoise and macedoine.
3. Explain the term 'segmenting'.
4. What happens to pastry that has been over handled?

👨‍🍳 Service chef!

1. Quiche Lorraine.
2. Bakewell tart.
3. Cheesy tuna fishcakes.
4. Spicy chicken and apricot tagine with couscous.

📁 Portfolio

Make these dishes well and photograph them as evidence for your portfolio.

Topic 2: Turn the heat up

Why do we cook food?

There are four main reasons for cooking food:

1. To improve the texture.
2. To improve the flavour.
3. To kill bacteria.
4. To make it easier to digest.

Cooking involves applying heat to a food, which results in a change to its structure, appearance and taste. There are different methods of applying heat to food and the way in which this heat travels through the food is known as '**heat transfer**'. Heat transfer happens in three ways:

- **Conduction:** heat is transferred through a solid surface directly onto a cold surface, e.g. frying a steak in a frying pan. The heat travels from the burner/ring up through the surface of the pan to the surface of the steak.

- **Convection:** heat is transferred through air or water/liquid. For example, when cooking roast beef, the air circulates around the beef in the oven, causing it to cook.

- **Radiation:** a direct heat transfers onto the surface of the food. For example, when grilling bacon the powerful heat from the grill falls directly onto the surface of the food. The food however must be turned over to allow it to cook on both sides.

Conduction, convection and radiation

Dry methods of cooking

A dry method of cookery does not involve the use of a liquid, e.g. baking, grilling, shallow frying.

Baking

All types of food can be baked e.g. poultry, lean meat, vegetables, fruit but some may require special care and protection from the heat.

Health benefits: Fruit and vegetables such as apples and potatoes can be baked without any additional fat. Potatoes when baked offer a **healthy alternative** to chips.

As well as bread, baking is used to prepare cakes, pastries, pies, tarts, quiches, cookies and scones. These popular items are known collectively as **'baked good'** and are sold at a bakery.

Health benefits: Loss of nutrients is minimal as the food is served as a whole – water soluble vitamins are not lost.

🔍 Hint

When baking you should always pre-heat the oven so that it is the correct temperature when the food is placed in the oven.

❓ Did you know?

In some establishments they have additional ovens, such as a pizza oven or large Gastronom ovens that can also be used for steaming foods as well as baking foods.

The methods of heat transfer during baking are:

* **conduction** through the pan and the oven shelf
* **convection** from the hot air circulating around the food.

Grilling

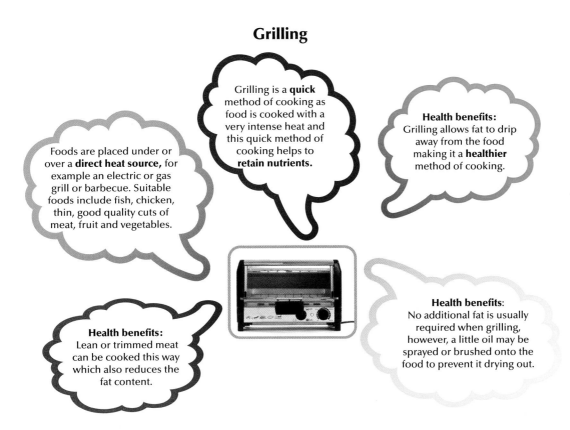

Grilling is a **quick** method of cooking as food is cooked with a very intense heat and this quick method of cooking helps to **retain nutrients.**

Foods are placed under or over a **direct heat source,** for example an electric or gas grill or barbecue. Suitable foods include fish, chicken, thin, good quality cuts of meat, fruit and vegetables.

Health benefits: Grilling allows fat to drip away from the food making it a **healthier** method of cooking.

Health benefits: Lean or trimmed meat can be cooked this way which also reduces the fat content.

Health benefits: No additional fat is usually required when grilling, however, a little oil may be sprayed or brushed onto the food to prevent it drying out.

? Did you know?

Charcoal cookery is the most ancient of cooking methods, and is still the most common way of cooking in Mediterranean and tropical climates. Roasting an animal over an open fire has always been a way of feasting in all places and eras. In its modern form, outdoor cookery is known as barbecue and has become more of a leisure activity. Some barbecues operate with lava stone heated by gas or solar energy however the most common fuel is wood charcoal.

The main method of **heat transfer** during grilling is **radiation**, where heat is directly radiated onto the surface of the food.

A **salamander grill** is an industrial appliance used for overhead grilling of steaks, fish, sausages, etc. and it can also be used for 'flash heating' and browning of dishes prior to serving.

A contact grill is used for grilling the top and bottom of the food at the same time. It cooks both sides evenly and the grill plates can be varied depending upon what is being cooked, e.g. ribbed plates or panini plates.

⌕ Hint

'Fat-reducing' grills have been developed to allow the fat to drip down from the grill plates into a specially designed tray on the front of the grill.

Shallow frying

Food is cooked in a pre-heated pan or a metal surface, with a small amount of fat or oil.

Foods that are **shallow fried** need to be turned in the pan to make sure they are evenly cooked.

Stir frying involves preparing foods, e.g. vegetables, meat, chicken, by cutting them into small, even-sized pieces before cooking them in a small amount of oil for a very short time.

Shallow frying is a fast method of cooking and is suitable for certain food that can be cooked quickly such as steaks, bacon, eggs and fish.

Health benefits: In stir frying the vegetables are cooked quickly so most water soluble vitamins such as vitamin C and B complex are retained. Only a small amount of oil is used. The use of a non-stick wok or frying pan will also cut down the fat content.

Sweat is the term given to cooking vegetables gently without browning in a little oil in either a frying pan or heavy based saucepan with a lid on.

Sauté is the term used to cook meat, fish or vegetables uncovered, in a little oil in a frying pan, sauté pan or heavy based saucepan. Sautéing browns the food's surface. It seals and develops the flavour in the food.

🔍 Hint

Shallow frying food at too low a temperature will cause the food to become greasy as it will absorb the fat.

The method of **heat transfer** in shallow frying is:

- **conduction** through the action of the heat from the burner or cooker ring through the pan to heat the oil and food
- **convection** through the movement of the oil around the food.

There are many different styles of frying pans, such as:

- omelette pan, a specially shaped pan with curved sides
- sauté pan, which has vertical sides and is good for meat
- sauteuse pan, which has sloping sides for reducing sauces
- wok, which is a Chinese pan used for stir-frying

Wet methods of cooking

A wet method of cooking involves using water or another liquid, e.g. boiling, poaching, steaming, stewing.

Boiling

Boiling involves cooking food in a **liquid**, such as water or stock. Sometimes chefs add wine and beer to the liquid to enhance the flavour.

Liquids are sometimes boiled to reduce them, as boiling causes liquid to **evaporate**.

Boiling can be a **quick** method of cooking for foods such as potatoes, pasta and eggs. It can also be a **longer, slower process,** when the heat is reduced from boiling point to **simmering**. The food is then cooked slowly and steadily in a sauce or liquid just below boiling point. This is good for tougher cuts of meat.

Boiling occurs at a fixed temperature, which for water is **100°C**. The boiling point of sugar syrup can be much higher than this.

Health benefits: Boiling does not involve the use of fat. The addition of salt can also be controlled.

The method of **heat transfer** for boiling is:

- **conduction** through the action of the heat, from the burner or cooker ring through the pot to heat the liquid and food
- convection through the movement of the liquid around the food.

? Did you know?

If a recipe contains an instruction to 'boil rapidly', this means that the ingredients should be agitated to prevent them sticking to each other or to the bottom of the pan.

🔍 Hint

The liquid used to cook the food in is often referred to as the cooking medium.

Poaching

Little or **no movement** from the cooking liquid is required as this prevents delicate foods such as eggs and fish breaking up.

Poaching involves cooking foods gently just below boiling point (usually **73–93°C**) in a liquid. It is important that food is monitored regularly and it is not boiled.

Pots and pans are usually used for poaching, however, a fish kettle is a specially designed piece of equipment for poaching whole fish.

This method of cooking is **gentle**, which helps the food being poached to retain its shape.

Health benefits: The cooking medium in poaching is generally water, but stock, milk or wine may be used instead. No fat is addded.

? Did you know?

- Deep poaching is where food is fully covered in the minimum amount of liquid and gently cooked, e.g. whole fish, eggs, pears.
- Shallow poaching is where the food is partly covered with liquid and gently cooked under cover in an oven, e.g. fillets of fish.

⌕ Hint

Poached eggs are often cooked and kept chilled in ice water. They are then reheated for service.

The method of **heat transfer** during poaching is:

- **conduction**, through the action of the heat from the burner or cooker ring through the pot to heat the liquid and food.
- convection through the movement of the liquid around the food.

Steaming

Steaming is a **gentle process** and care needs to be taken not to **overcook** the food.

Prepared food is cooked in **steam**. The water is heated to **100°C** to produce steam. Suitable foods include fish, chicken, vegetables, sweet puddings.

Pressure cookers can be used to steam foods as they can reach a higher temperature which cooks food more quickly.

The cooking **medium** in steaming is usually water.

Steamed food does not come into direct contact with water but is cooked in the steam rising from boiling water. Two popular ways are:
1. plate method e.g. fish
2. saucepan method e.g. puddings.

Health benefits:
Steaming is a healthy method of cooking as no fat is needed and there is little loss of nutrients such as vitamin C and B complex as the food does not come in direct contact with the water.

Hint: You can also steam frozen vegetables without defrosting them first.

The method of **heat transfer** during steaming is:

- **conduction**, through the action of the heat from the burner or cooker ring through the pot to heat water and food.

- **convection**, through the movement of the steam around the food.

Types of steamers

There are different items of equipment that can be used for steaming.

1. A saucepan with a small amount of water and a wire basket and tight fitting lid.

2. A special steaming saucepan, with an insert.

3. A commercial steamer, which is used in commercial kitchens to cook large amounts of food quickly at a higher temperature.

A commercial steamer

? Did you know?

Mushiki is the name of a round steamer made from bamboo, like those used in Chinese cuisine. Multi-stacked bamboo steamers will enable a variety of appetisers, vegetables and other kinds of food to be all cooked at once.

🔍 Hint

Care must be taken when steaming food as it can get extremely hot. A good tip is to place a folded strip of tinfoil under a steaming bowl to help lower and remove the bowl from the pan.

4. Electric steamers specifically designed for use in the home.
5. Bamboo steamers specifically used for Asian cuisine

A bamboo steamer

Stewing

A **stew** is a combination of solid **food ingredients** such as meat, poultry with vegetables that have been **cooked in liquid** and served in the resultant **gravy**. Fruit such as apples, rhubarb can also be stewed.

Stewing is a good method for cooking **tougher cuts of meat** as it is a longer and slower process.

Stewing is generally done in a **heavy based pan with a tight fitting lid**. The temperature should be **just below boiling point (simmering).**

Stews may be thickened by reduction or with flour, either by coating pieces of meat with flour before searing, or by using a roux or beurre manié (a dough consisting of equal parts of butter and flour). Thickeners like cornstarch or arrowroot may also be used.

There are **two types** of stews:
1. **Brown stew** – the end product is brown in colour, e.g. beef stew.
2. **White stew** – the end product is white/blond in colour, e.g. chicken fricassé.

Health benefits: Serving the liquid helps to **retain nutrients** such as water soluble vitamins C and B complex that may have leached out of the food into the liquid during the cooking process.

🔍 Hint

A stew needs to be checked regularly during cooking to ensure it does not stick to the base of the pan and that there is enough liquid.

The method of **heat transfer** during stewing is:

- **conduction**, through the action of the heat from the burner or cooker ring through the pot to heat water and food.
- **convection**, through the movement of the hot liquid around the food.

? Did you know?

Casseroling is the name used when food is started on the hob then transferred to the oven to finish the cooking process.

☑ Chef's test

Complete the following:

1. Describe the difference between a wet and a dry method of cooking and give examples of each.
2. What is a cooking medium?
3. Which method of cookery would you recommend for tougher cuts of meat and why?
4. Explain the process of poaching.
5. Select two healthy methods of cooking and for each explain why they are healthy.

👨‍🍳 Service chef!

Time to make a dish using some of the cookery processes. Examples of dishes you could make:

1. Poached pears with raspberry coulis or chocolate sauce.
2. Apple flan.
3. Carrot and courgette soup.
4. Grillsticks with a sour cream and chive dip.

📁 Portfolio

Make these dishes well and photograph them as evidence for your portfolio.

Topic 3: Testing for readiness

It is essential for a chef to judge when a food is properly cooked. This skill gets easier with experience; however, to help get it right there are certain tools available such as temperature probes.

Temperature probe

How to get it right

Vegetables

Root vegetables such as potatoes, turnips and onions should feel soft when firm pressure is applied. The food should be easily pierced with a fork – no force should be required.

Vegetables that grow above the ground such as broccoli, beans and cauliflower should have a crisp but tender texture when ready. The vegetables should resist being pierced with a fork.

Meat

Steak should be cooked to the customer's request.

- **Very rare (blue):** sealed for a few seconds only on each side.
- **Rare:** meat has a reddish tinge and is often referred to as 'bleeding'.
- **Medium:** the meat has a slight pinkness but no blood should be running from the steak.
- **Well done:** the meat is thoroughly cooked and there is no pink colour.

Lamb may also be served 'on the pink', but all other types of meat, such as pork, must be thoroughly cooked.

Poultry

The outer skin of a roast should be dark golden in colour and when pierced with a skewer between the legs and carcass the juices should run clear. It is important to cook poultry properly to prevent food poisoning.

Fish

Fish can be tested in three ways.

1. By using a knife – a thin bladed knife should pass easily through the thickest part.
2. By sight – the flesh of the skin should be opaque. If it is translucent it is not cooked.
3. The flesh of the fish should 'flake' or come away easily from the bone.

Pasta

The best way to test pasta is to remove a piece from the pan and taste it. It should look slightly swollen with water and still have a little bite when eaten. This is called 'al dente'.

Hint

If the cooking water starts to turn cloudy, this can be a sign that the pasta is getting overcooked.

Rice

Remove a grain of rice and taste it. It should feel soft with no hard or grainy parts. It can also be tested by squeezing a grain between the fingers – it should be soft.

Hint

The rice grains should be swollen but should not 'burst'.

Baking

Cakes should be golden-brown and spring back when the surface is pressed lightly with the fingertips. The cake should also be starting to shrink back from the sides of the tin. For larger cakes it is advisable to pierce the cake with a metal skewer or cocktail stick and check if it comes out clean.

Hint

Never open the oven door too soon as the cold air will cause the cake to sink.

Bread

Bread should be golden-brown in colour and when the base is tapped it should sound 'hollow'. It can also be tested by piercing a skewer into the thickest part of the loaf and it should come out clean.

Hint

Scones should also sound 'hollow' when the underside is tapped.

Egg whites

Egg whites should be tested for readiness during both preparation and cooking.

- **Preparation:** when whisking it is important to ensure the whites form peaks before adding any sugar. If egg whites are under whipped they will not hold their shape. It is important to make sure that no water or egg yolk comes into contact with egg whites as this will prevent it from whisking. A good way to test if egg whites are whisked enough is to tip the bowl slightly to one side – the mixture should not move in the bowl.

- **Cooking:** depending on the type of finish required, the meringue should be cooked slowly at a very low temperature so that it is completely dried out. However when making a pavlova, the centre of the meringue should be slightly softer. The meringue mixture on a lemon meringue pie can be cooked at a higher temperature to set and brown the surface while keeping the centre of the meringue soft.

Cream

Cream must be tested for readiness during preparation to see if it is the correct consistency for piping or spreading. When the cream starts to thicken, it is important to stop beating vigorously. Lift the beaters out of the bowl to test the consistency. For 'soft peak' the cream should rise up a little and the tip of the peak should fall slightly to one side and for 'stiff peak' the tip of the peak should hold its shape and stay upright.

Hint

It is very easy to over-whip cream. If this happens it will separate and turn to butter and cannot be used.

✔ Chef's test

Complete the following:

1. Describe three ways to test fish for readiness.
2. What happens to cream that is over-whipped?
3. Explain how to test a sponge for readiness.
4. What does the term 'al dente' mean and which food should be served this way?

🎩 Service chef!

Time to test for readiness with the following dishes:

1. Mini Lemon Bakewell Tarts.
2. Spicy Chicken Risotto.
3. Macaroni and Beef Bake.
4. Mini Chocolate-Dipped Meringues.

Hint

A successful chef will make sure that garnishes/ decorations not only enhance the look of the dish, but complement the flavour and colour of the dish as well, e.g. a tomato and basil pasta dish could be garnished with a sprig of fresh basil.

Topic 4: All in the finish

First impressions of a dish are the most important as many people **'eat with their eyes'** so to speak. Ask yourself how many times you have had a plate of food that looks extremely appetising but doesn't live up to expectations once tasted. Or, how many times you have had a plate of food that doesn't look very pleasant but tastes fantastic. The secret is to get the balance of both right.

Garnishing/decoration and portion control are essential if a dish is to be successful.

Simple tips for garnishing/decorating:

Garnishes and decorations can be very complicated or very simple, however, they should always be:

- Edible and served as fresh as possible.
- The correct size in relation to the foods being served.
- A flavour in keeping with the food. If too highly seasoned, it will take away from the flavour of the dish.
- Neatly arranged in a way that will enhance the food.

The ABC of garnishing tools

It is important to use the correct equipment when preparing a garnish or decoration. Some of the equipment can be quite standard, however, there are many more specialist pieces of equipment being developed all the time for this purpose.

- **Apple corer:** used to cut out small thin rounds from hard fruits and vegetables such as carrots and apples. There are now more small cutters available for this type of work.
- **Butter curler:** used to shape butter into delicate curls. This is also a good way of portioning butter. For ease of use, the butter should be hard and the butter curler should be dipped into hot water prior to shaping each curl.
- **Julienne peeler:** used to cut vegetables into thin, even-sized batons or strips. Julienne strips of carrot or beetroot can be used to garnish a salad.
- **Melon baller:** used to create small, even-sized balls of fruit or vegetables. Melon ballers can be bought in different sizes, or some have two different sizes in the one tool. It is good for garnishing a parma ham dish.

🔍 Hint

A garnish/decoration may also be used to indicate portioning of a food such as a cheesecake, gateau or savoury flan. For your exam you will be asked to portion one of the dishes to serve four people. The portion size and finish on the plates must be identical. It is a good idea to look at a plate and think of a clock, that way everything will be placed at the same point on each of the four plates. For example, a portion of the flan placed at 11 o'clock; a slice of tomato at 11.30, 8 and 3 o'clock; a bunch of salad leaves at 10 o'clock; and three slices of spring onion at 1.30.

Apple corer

Butter curler

Julienne peeler

Melon baller

Zester

- **Zester**: used to remove thin, even strips from the skin or flesh of fruit and vegetables, in particular citrus fruits. The strips removed from citrus fruits can be used in the recipe to enhance the flavour. The strips of zest can be blanched and used to decorate dishes e.g. citrus cheesecake.

Garnishes and decorations should not be used to disguise deficiencies or food of poor quality and it is better to use fresh garnishes and decorations. Garnishes should also be in proportion to the food being served.

A simple common garnish such as wedge of lemon would be appropriate for a fish dish as the lemon can be squeezed to enhance the flavour of the fish as well as adding colour to the plate of food. However, the same wedge of lemon would be inappropriate for a lemon cheesecake as it would not likely be squeezed onto the cheesecake. Sometimes **simple is effective**, e.g. a sprig of parsley, however, where you are looking for a garnish with '**flair**' more elements – at least two – are required e.g. a fantail strawberry with teardrops of fruit coulis.

The style of dish serves as an accessory to the food so the serving dish, as well as the garnish/decoration used, must be considered.

The ABC of garnishes

Grated chocolate

Chocolate curls

Chocolate run-outs

- **Chocolate** can be used to decorate many sweet dishes. It can be used in a variety of ways from grated through to chocolate curls and run-outs.
  - **Grated:** use a block of chocolate that is cold and firm and use a hand grater. It is a good idea to cut the chocolate up into smaller blocks for grating as this will prevent it from melting in the hands before being grated. It is also advisable to thoroughly wash and dry the grater surface at regular intervals as the chocolate will not grate properly if the blades become coated in chocolate.
  - **Curls:** use a vegetable peeler with a long narrow blade. Warm the blade and chocolate slightly then use the peeler to peel along the smooth surface of the chocolate to make curls.
  - **Melted chocolate** can be used to give swirls, drizzles, curls and chocolate shapes. To cut out shapes, smooth the melted chocolate over a piece of parchment paper. When the chocolate is just about set but still flexible, use cutters to make the desired shapes such as leaves, circles or hearts. Leave the chocolate shapes to completely set before removing from the parchment paper for use.

– **Chocolate run-outs:** make a paper piping bag first and fill with the melted chocolate. Snip the piping end with sharp scissors then pipe shapes onto parchment paper. Allow to set completely before removing.

- **Coulis:** A form of thick sauce made from puréed and strained vegetables or fruits. A vegetable coulis is commonly used on meat and vegetable dishes, and it can also be used as a base for soups or other sauces. Fruit coulis is most often used on desserts or to decorate the dessert plate. Raspberry coulis, for example, is especially popular with poached pears. A simple way to form a teardrop effect is to place half a teaspoon of coulis on the plate then drag either the end of the teaspoon or a cocktail stick out from the centre of the coulis.

> **🔍 Hint**
> Don't make the chocolate shapes too thin as they will break easily. It is also a good idea to draw the shape on the underside of the paper as a template.

> **🔍 Hint**
> Visit the following website to see how to make a paper piping bag: www.youtube.com/watch?v=-yMqLYkY5hE.

A dessert decorated with chocolate run outs and coulis

- **Cream:** Whipped cream can also be piped onto a food or plate and then decorated with a sprig of mint, slice of fruit or a chocolate run-out.

- **Lemon:** Lemons are a popular garnish with fish dishes. They are usually sliced or made into wedges for garnishing the plate, however, there are other ways of presenting lemon such as:
  - Van Dyke
  - Lemon wedges with a difference
  - Lemon butterfly
  - Citrus loop

Lemon butterfly

Van Dyke

Lemon wedges with a difference

Citrus loop

Segmeting an orange

Orange wedges

- **Orange segments:** remove the skin and pith with a knife and then separate the inner membranes.
  - To do this you must carry out the following stages:
    - **i.** Remove a slice from the top and the bottom of the orange – this provides a flat base.
    - **ii.** Cut the outer skin from the flesh, working from the top to the bottom. It is important to follow the natural shape of the orange and to remove only the outer skin and pith without removing excess flesh of the orange.
    - **iii.** Remove any remaining pith before cutting out each segment between the inner membrane.
  - When removing the segments, place a bowl under the orange to catch any of the juice, and when finished squeeze out any remaining juice from the orange that is left. This can be used for another dish.
  - Oranges can also be sliced or cut into wedges
- **Parsley** is an example of a traditional garnish; this pungent green herb has small distinctly shaped leaves, firm stems, and is easy to trim into a simple but effective garnish that adds both colour and flavour to a dish. There are two types, flat leaf and curled parsley, both of which can be used in two ways:
  - **Sprig** (parsley en branche). If using a sprig of parsley to garnish a dish, wash and dry it well in kitchen paper and remember to keep the sprig of parsley in proportion to the size of food being garnished.
  - **Chopped**. If using chopped parsley follow the following simple steps.
    - **i.** **"Dunk and swish"** the parsley in water.
      Put the parsley bunch in a bowl of cold water and swish it around; dirt will fall to the bottom of the bowl.
    - **ii.** **"Shake off excess water"**
      Remove parsley from bowl and shake off excess water.
    - **iii.** **"Pat the leaves dry"**
      Place parsley on a clean paper towel and pat parsley.
    - **iv.** **"Pick the leaves from the stem"**
      Carefully remove the leaves from the stem and remember only take off as much as you plan to use immediately.

v. Chop or "slice" the parsley

Gather the leaves into a pile, and slice roughly. Remember to use a sharp knife as a blunt knife will bruise the leaves.

vi. Rock the knife back and forth for a finer chop

For a finer chop, use one hand to hold the tip of the knife on the cutting board while the other hand rocks the knife down and across the leaves and continue until the parsley reaches is the desired size.

- Other herbs, such as coriander and basil, can be prepared in a similar way.

- **Spring onion curls** can be prepared as follows:

    i. Trim the bulbs (white part) from the onions; reserve for another use, if desired. Trim remaining stems (green part) to 10 cm lengths.

    ii. Using sharp scissors, cut each section of green stems lengthwise into very thin strips down to the beginning of the stems, cutting 6–8 strips from each stem section.

    iii. Fill a large bowl about half-full with cold water. Add the spring onions and ice cubes. Refrigerate until the onions curl (about 1 hour) then drain.

- **Strawberry fantail:** slice the strawberry from the stalk end, making sure not to cut through the stalk. Carefully fan the strawberry out.

- There are many other ways of using strawberries to decorate a dish, examples of which can be found on the internet, in recipe books and food magazines.

- **Tomatoes** can simply be sliced or cut into wedges, however, the skin can be thinly peeled and rolled into a tomato rose or it can be made into a **tomato concassé**.

    - The tomato is peeled, seeded (seeds and skins removed) and then chopped to specified dimensions such as rough chop, small dice, medium dice, or large dice.

    - The most popular use for tomato concassé is in an Italian bruschetta, typically in a small dice concassé mixed with olive oil and fresh basil, and sometimes other ingredients such as onion, olives, or anchovies. However, many chefs also like to use a small dice to garnish plates.

🔍 Hint

Only prepare parsley just before service to prevent it wilting and discolouring.

Spring onion curls

Strawbery fantail

🔍 Hint

Watch the video Tomato Concassé by Stephane Sauthier: www.youtube.com/watch?v=q-dOd56WriI

Step 1: *Cut an X on the bottom of the tomato.*

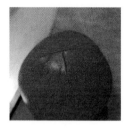

Step 2: *Place the tomato in boiling water.*

Step 3: *Remove the tomato after 30 seconds.*

Step 4: *Plunge the tomato into ice-cold water.*

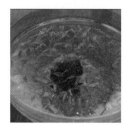

Step 5: *Transfer the cooled tomato to a chopping board.*

Step 6: *Peel the tomato skin off the flesh of the tomato.*

Step 7: *Cut the tomato into quarters and remove the seeds.*

Step 8: *Square off the edges and dice to required size.*

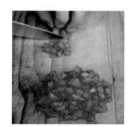

✔ Chef's test

Complete the following:

1. Explain the difference between a garnish and a decoration.
2. Describe how to segment an orange.
3. Describe three ways of using chocolate as a decoration.
4. Explain the stages of chopping parsley.
5. What should a garnish/decoration add to a dish?

👨‍🍳 Service chef!

Time to make a dish using some of the techniques. Examples of dishes you could make are:

1. Orange Cheesecake decorated with segments of orange.
2. Chocolate and Strawberry Gateau decorated with fantail strawberries and chocolate.
3. Mackerel Pâté garnished with lemon.
4. Prepare a concassé of tomato and use as basis for a tomato salsa.

📁 Portfolio

Make these dishes well and photograph them as evidence for your portfolio.

GO! End of chapter activities

Activity 1

Working on your own

Investigate each of the food preparation techniques mentioned on page 000 in more detail. Use the information to make up a chef's notebook of tips and techniques to use in the hospitality industry.

Activity 2

Working on your own

Design a fridge magnet that could be stuck to the fridge of a catering kitchen to remind chefs of the cuts of vegetables.

Activity 3

As a class

Watch the following videos:

- 'How to Pipe the Perfect Cupcake Swirl': www.youtube.com/watch?v=kn8a3cJD8Qg
- 'How to Line a Flan Case with Pastry': http://www.youtube.com/watch?v=HOaV6YGX6IQ.

Activity 4

Working on your own

Divide a paper plate into five sections and label each one with the names of the different cuts of vegetables.

(continued)

Now peel a carrot and cut it up using the five different cuts. Place each of your cuts in the correct section and you could take a photograph of your work.

As a class

Evaluate each student's cuts and give them a score out of 10.

Activity 5

Working on your own

Design and produce a leaflet for an up and coming chef entitled 'How to decorate and garnish a dish'. The leaflet should include details of how to prepare garnishes and decorations. Use illustrations where possible.

Activity 6

Working on your own

Complete this wordsearch.

Food preparation techniques

S	I	E	V	E	V	G	D	A	H	P	K	U	I
C	U	T	K	F	J	E	N	I	W	U	O	R	B
Q	H	E	R	O	P	S	E	S	C	R	W	U	A
R	V	O	P	I	C	X	L	K	N	E	A	D	K
O	T	Y	P	O	M	W	B	T	A	E	B	P	E
L	D	S	A	F	H	I	K	A	H	L	O	L	B
L	I	N	E	S	E	L	X	O	D	P	D	I	L
O	S	C	A	M	A	E	R	C	N	X	S	H	I
U	J	W	H	I	S	K	A	F	O	L	D	I	N
T	E	E	Y	I	R	T	H	M	C	E	M	F	D
H	R	I	D	F	N	E	K	U	I	E	B	O	T
O	T	G	R	A	T	E	S	H	A	P	E	S	L
K	A	H	B	N	E	V	L	A	B	B	D	N	E
F	U	O	S	L	I	C	E	R	U	S	A	E	M

GO! Activity

WEIGH	BLEND	MIX	ROLL OUT	PEEL	PUREE
WHISK	BAKE BLIND	DICE	MEASURE	BEAT	MELT
KNEAD	CUT	FOLD IN	CREAM	LINE	CHOP
WASH	COAT	SIEVE	SHAPE	SLICE	PIPE
TRIM	GRATE				

Rate Your Progress

How confident are you that you have achieved each of the following objectives?

Using the following key as a guide, give yourself a rating for each of the objectives below.

Rating	Explanation
1	Confident with the standard of my work.
2	Fairly confident with the standard of my work.
3	The majority of my work was satisfactory.
4	Require to do some further work.
5	Require a lot of work.

Objectives	Rating
Select and use equipment to weigh and measure ingredients accurately.	
Apply a range of food preparation techniques using appropriate equipment with precision.	
Cook prepared ingredients according to recipes.	
Control the stages of the cookery processes and testing food for readiness.	
Present and garnish or decorate the dishes and, where appropriate, portion them.	
Work safely and hygienically.	

Looking at your ratings

Write down two next steps to 'unlocking' your knowledge of cookery skills, techniques and processes.

What's this unit all about?

This unit will develop your knowledge and understanding of ingredients from a variety of different sources and of their characteristics. It also examines the importance of sustainability, responsible sourcing of ingredients and current dietary advice. This will give you knowledge to help you in selecting and using a range of ingredients during practical food preparation.

By the end of this unit you should be able to:

1. **Outcome 1: Apply an understanding of ingredients from a range of categories.** This means you have to:

    1.1 Identify a variety of ingredients and their characteristics

    1.2 Describe and demonstrate safe and appropriate storage methods for ingredients

    1.3 Describe how current dietary advice influences the selection, preparation, and use of ingredients

    1.4 Describe the importance of sourcing sustainable ingredients

2. **Outcome 2: Use ingredients in the preparation of dishes.** This means you have to:

    2.1 Select, prepare and/or cook the ingredients according to recipes

    2.2 Demonstrate specialist garnishing and/or decorating techniques

    2.3 Work safely and hygienically

UNIT 2
Understanding and Using Ingredients

3 Plate it up!

By the end of this chapter you should be able to:

- Describe how current dietary advice influences the selection, preparation and use of ingredients.
- Select, prepare and/or cook the ingredients according to recipes.
- Demonstrate specialist garnishing and/or decorating techniques.
- Work safely and hygienically.

Topic 1: What's on your plate?

With the rates of obesity, heart disease, high blood pressure, diabetes and cancer rising, it is important to eat well at home and to have the option of a healthy choice when eating out. The UK hospitality industry can help customers to make healthier choices by ensuring that through menus, counter and buffet displays, healthy food and drink choices are highlighted.

By promoting: ✓	By reducing: ✗	By providing: ✓
• eating five fruits and vegetables per day • fresh fish on menus to include oily fish • healthier methods of cooking, such as stir frying • starchy foods, particularly whole grain varieties	• the amount of salt in cooking • the saturated fats and sugars in our foods	• calorie/energy information on menus and websites • nutritional information on menus and websites

Using the 'eatwell plate' as a guide could help people with portion control and to follow a balanced and nutritious diet.

Eat Well Plate

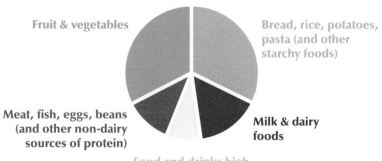

Fruit & vegetables

Bread, rice, potatoes, pasta (and other starchy foods)

Meat, fish, eggs, beans (and other non-dairy sources of protein)

Milk & dairy foods

Food and drinks high in fat and/or sugar

The different size of the sections in the plate shows that there are some foods you can eat more of, such as fruit and vegetables, bread, rice, potatoes and pasta, but you should limit the intake of fatty and sugary foods.

Current dietary advice and the selection, preparation and use of ingredients

The following **top tips** should help both the customer and chef to encourage healthy choices.

🔍 **Hint**

Some **top tips** will apply to more than one eatwell plate section.

Fruit and vegetables

NUTRIENT NEWS

- Fruit and vegetables are sources of vitamins A, C, E, which are anti-oxidant vitamins.
- Green vegetables and dried fruit contain iron.
- Some vegetables contain B vitamins, including folic acid.
- Fruit and vegetables are low in calories.
- Almost all fruit and vegetables are fat-free.

NEWS EXTRA
They also are a good source of fibre, especially if the skins are eaten.

You should try to have at least **five portions** of fruit and vegetables each day, but **what is a portion**?

- 150 ml unsweetened fruit juice
- Three heaped tablespoons of vegetables or fruit salad (approximately 80 g)
- A handful of grapes, cherries or berries
- One banana, apple, orange or two plums or similar sized fruit
- One bowl of salad
- One bowl of home-made soup
- One tablespoon of dried fruit

Here are some **top tips** for serving fruit and vegetables.

- Serve salads without dressings – offer dressings as an additional extra so that customers can decide if they wish to add it.
- Salad dressings should be low in fat.
- Two types of vegetables or salad, not including potatoes, should be offered with each main meal.
- Serve sauces based on tomatoes or vegetables instead of creamy or cheese sauces.
- Use a variety of vegetables in soups – soups can be liquidised to encourage customer choice.
- Frozen vegetables are convenient as they can be stored and are just as nutritious, or sometimes even more so, than fresh.
- Offer fresh fruit as a breakfast or dessert option.
- Smoothies are a good way of using a variety of fruit and are a good way of getting children to eat fruit.
- Add dried fruit such as apricots, cranberries, sultanas to baking, breakfast cereals and desserts.

Bread, rice, potatoes, pasta and other starchy foods

NUTRIENT NEWS

- Bread, rice, potatoes and pasta are sources of complex carbohydrates.
- They are low in fat but watch what you add to them and how they are cooked!
- Calcium and iron are added to bread to 'fortify' it.
- Vitamin B complex

NEWS EXTRA
Bread, rice, potatoes and pasta are also good sources of fibre, especially if wholegrain varieties are eaten.

You should try to have at least **two portions** of this group at each meal, but **what is a portion?**

- One bowl of wholegrain breakfast cereal
- One slice of bread – preferably wholemeal or wholegrain
- One medium potato – but not in the form of chips or roast potatoes
- Two tablespoon of cooked rice or pasta – preferably the wholemeal variety

Here are some **top tips** for serving rice, potatoes and pasta (and other starchy foods).

- Breakfast cereals should be high fibre, low sugar varieties. These can also be used in toppings for desserts such as fruit crumbles or biscuits, e.g. porridge oats.
- Use wholemeal flour when cooking and baking instead of white.
- Wholemeal varieties of breads, pitta breads, granary rolls and bagels should be easily available to the customer.
- Potatoes should be baked, or boiled with the skin on.
- If potatoes are mashed, use low fat spreads/polyunsaturated spreads and skimmed/semi-skimmed milk.
- Baked potato wedges are a healthier option than chips.
- Where chips are on the menu, customers should also have the option of a healthier alternative such as baked or boiled potatoes.
- Serve rice boiled or steamed and use brown rice if possible. Avoid fried rice such as pilau and egg fried rice.
- Add pasta or rice to soups to make them more filling.
- Use tomato-based sauces with pasta.

Hint

This is an example of how this **top tip** links to more than one plate section i.e fruit and vegetables.

Meat, fish, eggs, beans (and other non-dairy sources of protein)

NUTRIENT NEWS

- Meat, fish, eggs and beans are sources of protein.
- White fish, chicken and turkey are lower in fat.
- Oily fish such as salmon will supply omega 3 and vitamins A and D.
- Meat supplies the vitamin B complex.
- Red meats contain iron.
- Fish where the bones are eaten, e.g. tinned salmon, are good sources of calcium and phosphorous.
- Pulses including lentils, beans such as kidney, butter and soya, and peas are low in fat, high in fibre, contain iron and add extra protein.
- Meat alternatives such as mycoprotein (QuornTM), tofu and textured vegetable protein are low in fat and good sources of fibre.

You should try to have **two portions daily**, but **what is a portion?**

- 60 g cooked lean meat or poultry
- 90 g cooked fish
- Two eggs
- 90 g beans

Here are some **top tips** for serving meat, fish, eggs, beans (and other non-dairy sources of protein).

- Use lean cuts of meat, extra-lean minced beef or trim the excess fat from meat.
- Remove the skin from poultry before cooking to reduce fat.
- Include more fish on the menu:
  - steam, poach or bake fish instead of coating in batter or creamy sauces
  - include as a starter or a main course.
- Boil, poach or scramble eggs instead of frying them.
- Add pulses to meat dishes to increase the fibre content, reduce the fat and add extra protein.

Milk and dairy

NUTRIENT NEWS

Milk and dairy are sources of:

- **Protein**
- **Calcium**
- **Vitamins A and D**

You should try to have **two or three portions** daily, but **what is a portion?**

- 200 ml milk
- 125 ml yoghurt
- 30 g cheese
- 50 ml cream, fromage frais, crème fraîche.

Here are some **top tips** for serving milk and dairy.

- Use lower fat versions of this food group, such as semi-skimmed or skimmed milk and low fat yoghurts, cream, fromage frais or crème fraîche.
- Use low fat plain yoghurt, fromage frais or crème fraîche instead of cream or sour cream in recipes.
- Serve plain instead of fruit yoghurt, which allows customers to add their choice of fresh fruit.
- Offer low fat spreads in addition to butter for spreading.
- If using cheese to flavour a dish, use a very strong-tasting cheese such as Red Leicester or blue cheese, because less is needed.
- Offer reduced-fat cheese, edam cheese or cottage cheese for salads or cheeseboards.

 Hint

Read the label carefully e.g. when selecting yoghurt, as many versions especially the low fat ones can contain up to four teaspoons of sugar in a carton.

Foods and drinks high in fat and/or sugar

Foods containing fats and sugars are often eaten in greater quantities than is needed by the body.

Fat

Here are some **top tips** for reducing fat in foods.

- Choose a cookery method that does not require extra fat, such as grilling, steaming, baking, poaching.
- Use spray olive oil when sweating vegetables or use a non-stick pan.
- If food is fried, make sure the oil is at the correct temperature as this reduces the amount of fat that is absorbed, and use kitchen paper to soak up any excess fat or oil.
- Use unsaturated oils such as olive, sunflower or rapeseed oils in preference to other oils when cooking.
- Skim fat from stews, soups before serving.
- Offer a low fat spread or a polyunsaturated fat instead of butter in pre-packed portions.
- Use fat-free or reduced calorie salad dressings.
- Change the pastry topping of a savoury pie to mashed potato.

Sugar

Here are some **top tips** for reducing sugar in foods.

- Serve alternatives to sugary drinks, such as water and unsweetened fruit juices.
- Provide artificial sweeteners for use in tea or coffee.
- Avoid serving sugar-coated breakfast cereals.
- Always have fresh fruit on offer.
- Reduce the amount of sugar used in some dishes and add spices such as cinnamon, mixed spice or cloves instead.

Remember salt!

Salt is found in many foods on the eatwell plate, for example in breads, cereals, cheese and in a wide variety of processed foods. Here are some **top tips** for reducing salt in foods.

- Use herbs and spices to flavour foods instead of salt.
- Always taste food before adding salt. This can be during the cooking process or before serving.
- Provide reduced-salt versions of foods, e.g. baked beans.
- Make your own stock using vegetables or use reduced-salt stock cubes.

- Limit the use of soy sauce or change to reduced-salt soy sauce for stir frying.
- Offer low sodium salt as an alternative.

? Did you know?

Using some of these top tips will result in healthier choices without affecting the taste of foods. So remember you can either:

- **Reduce the amount of ingredients,** e.g. use less oil when sautéing vegetables.
- **Make a healthy substitution,** e.g. use herbs instead of salt.
- **Change the method of cooking,** e.g. frying to grilling.

👨‍🍳 Chef's test

Complete the following:

1. List two ways to reduce salt when cooking.
2. Investigate the effect on health of the following nutrients: protein, iron, calcium, folic acid, vitamin C, vitamin A and vitamin D. Use any suitable books to help you, or the British Nutrition Foundation website at http://www.nutrition.org.uk/healthyliving/basics/what-are-nutrients.
3. State five ways of including bread, rice, potatoes and pasta in a healthy choices menu.
4. Describe three ways you could encourage children to eat fruit and vegetables.
5. Identify the five main nutrients found in each section of the eatwell plate.
6. Look at the following recipe for a fruit crumble and make four suggestions on how to make it a healthier option. Give reasons for your suggestions.

Fruit Crumble	
Base	**Topping**
200 g cooking apples 50 g sugar	125 g plain flour 50 g margarine 50 g sugar 2.5 ml mixed spice

7. Go to the British Heart Foundation website, www.bhf.org.uk, and download or read the booklet called *Eating Well* for more hints and tips on healthy eating.

Service chef!

Prepare some dishes using the sections of the eatwell plate. Each recipe focuses on the main ingredients, but remember that food from other sections of the eatwell plate will also be in the recipes.

Section	Recipes
Fruit and vegetables	Apple and Cinnamon Parcels Vegetable Samosas Carrot and Courgette Soup
Bread, rice, potatoes and pasta	Bombay Potatoes
Meat, fish, eggs, beans	Chilli Meatballs with Rice
Milk and dairy	Fruit Brulée
Fatty and sugary foods	Lemon or Lime Meringue Pie Chocolate and Strawberry Gateau

Topic 2: Eating out

When people eat out, although they may not choose a 'healthy dish', there should always be a healthy option choice available on the menu for those who wish it. There is a likelihood of eating more fat, sugar and salty foods when you are not preparing food yourself. The hospitality industry is making considerable progress in offering a wider range of healthy options for those customers who wish to choose them.

Encouraging healthy choices – caterers

The healthyliving award (HLA) is a national award for the food service sector in Scotland. It rewards caterers for serving healthier food and helping their customers make better food choices.

healthyliving award
the sign of healthier food

The healthyliving award has been designed to make it easier to eat healthier food when eating out. Award holders across Scotland, such as cafes, sandwich shops, workplace restaurants, colleges and other places where you buy meals and snacks, are making changes to the way they prepare food.

Only places that are committed to preparing and serving food according to the award conditions can display the healthyliving award logo and certificate.

How can caterers achieve a healthyliving award?

- Levels of fats and oils, particularly saturated fat, must be kept to a minimum.
- Levels of salt must be kept to a minimum.

- Levels of sugar must be kept to a minimum.
- Fruit and vegetables must be clearly available.
- Starchy foods must form the main part of most meals.
- Where appropriate, healthy and nutritious children's food should be provided.
- At least 50% of the food on the menu must meet the specific healthy living criteria, and be prepared using both healthier ingredients and cooking methods.
- Caterers have a promotion and marketing strategy, which supports healthier eating.

The award forms an important part of the Scottish Government's aim to reduce overweight and obesity. Watch short videos of caterers who have achieved the healthyliving award talking about their experience of applying for the award and what it means to them and their business.

Visit http://www.youtube.com/user/healthylivingaward.

Encouraging healthy choices – customers

Often it is up to the customer to make sensible choices. The next pages show some examples of ways that customers could choose healthier options when eating out.

> **? Did you know?**
>
> Caterers can also apply for The Plus Award
>
> - The healthyliving award **plus** rewards catering establishments that demonstrate a greater commitment to supporting healthier eating. To be eligible to apply for this, caterers must have held the standard healthy living award for a full 2-year term.
> - Many food outlets provide nutritional information on their website. Other websites publish comparison nutrition guides or mobile apps for smart phones.

Italian cuisine	
Less-healthy choices	**Healthier choices**

Main courses
• Pizza: large deep-pan pizzas, pizzas with the crust stuffed with cheese, triple cheese with pepperoni pizzas.
• Pasta dishes: creamy or butter-based sauces such as carbonara.
 	
Accompaniments
• Breads: garlic bread, which often contains a lot of butter.
 	
	Main courses
	• Pizza
	  – Choose lower-fat toppings, such as vegetables, ham, fish and prawn
	  – A small or medium pizza with a thin base and vegetable or lean meat topping
	  – Pizzas with no cheese are becoming more widely available.
	• Pasta dishes: a sauce that's based on tomatoes or vegetables.
	
	Accompaniments
	• Breads:
	  – Bruschetta, which is a ciabatta bread toasted and topped with fresh tomatoes and herbs.
	  – Plain rolls or breadsticks.

Chinese cuisine	
Less-healthy choices	**Healthier choices**

Starters/main courses
• **Fried foods:** anything that's battered or marked as 'crispy' on the menu means it's deep fried.
  – Sweet and sour pork is usually battered.
  – Starters such as prawn crackers and spring rolls are generally deep fried.
Accompaniments
• Fried rice.
	Main courses
	• Stir fried foods: these are usually lower in fat and include vegetables e.g. chicken chop suey, Szechuan prawns.
	• **Steamed foods:** steamed dumplings, vegetables or fish.
	Accompaniments
	• Steamed brown rice or boiled rice.

Thai cuisine	
Less-healthy choices	**Healthier choices**
Starters • Fish cakes, spring rolls, satay skewers with peanut sauce. **Main courses** • Thai curries, such as green and red curries, contain coconut milk, which is high in saturated fat. **Accompaniments** • Egg fried rice, prawn crackers.	**Starters** • Clear soups such as tom yum. **Main courses** • Choose stir-fried dishes or steamed dishes containing chicken, fish or vegetables instead of curries. **Accompaniments** • Steamed rice

Indian cuisine	
Less-healthy choices	**Healthier choices**
Main courses • Creamy curries such as korma, passanda or masala. **Accompaniments** • Pilau rice, naan, bhajis, pakoras and poppadoms.	**Main courses** • Dishes with tomato-based sauces, such as tandoori and madras with chicken, prawns or vegetables. **Accompaniments** • Plain rice or chapatti, plenty of vegetables, including lentil side dishes (known as dhal).

❓ Did you know?

Chinese and Indian dishes have been modified especially for the British palate, e.g. Chicken Tikka Masala. Unfortunately some of the modifications have resulted in the dishes being less healthy than the original versions.

Fast foods: kebab and burgers	
Less-healthy choices	**Healthier choices**

Main courses
 	
• Kebabs: doner kebabs can be high in fat. Try to avoid large doner kebabs with mayonnaise and no salad.
 	
• Burgers
  – Breaded or battered chicken or fish burgers.
  – Extra cheese or bacon and high-fat sauces such as mayonnaise.
  – Thin-cut chips.
	Main courses
	
	• Kebabs: choose a shish kebab, which is a skewer with whole cuts of meat or fish and usually grilled. Have it with pitta bread and salad,
	
	• Burgers
	  – Regular, single hamburger without mayo or cheese and have with extra salad or a baked potato instead of chips.
	  – Grilled burgers made from lean fish or meat (beef or whole chicken breast) and without cheese and mayonnaise.
	  – Vegetable burger.

👨‍🍳 Chef's test

Complete the following:

1. Explain why a customer might choose to eat at a restaurant that has achieved a healthyliving award.

2. How might a chef reduce the fat content of a) lasagne and b) cheesecake.

3. How could the fibre content be increased in the following:

   a) Ham sandwich made with white bread.

   b) Spaghetti Bolognese.

   c) Cheese and Tomato Pizza.

4. Take away fast food outlets are very popular. Produce an advice sheet on how to make healthier food choices from these outlets.

🔍 Hint

Remember 'super-sized' portions such as triple burgers or large portions of fries can lead to 'super-sized' people.

🔍 Hint

If you are having chips with your meal remember the thicker the chips the better because they absorb less fat. Try to have a smaller portion or share your chips!

❓ Did you know?

• Just because a food packet contains the words 'lower-fat' or 'reduced-fat', this doesn't necessarily mean it's a healthy choice.

• The lower-fat claim means that the food is 30% lower in fat than the standard version. So if the type of food is high in fat in the first place, the lower-fat version may also still be high in fat. For example, a lower-fat mayonnaise is 30% lower in fat than the standard version, but it is still high in fat. These foods may not be low in calories. Often the fat is replaced with sugar, and the food may end up with the same, or higher, calorie content.

Service chef!

Prepare some of the following healthier recipe choices, which you may see on a menu when eating out.

- **Italian** – Minestrone Soup, Chicken Cacciatora with pasta.
- **Chinese** – Sweet and Sour Chicken, Stir-Fried Pork with Noodles.
- **Indian** – Spicy Dahl and Carrot Soup, Chicken Balti with Boiled Rice.

GO! End of chapter activities

Activity 1

Working on your own

A businessman, who often has to stay in hotels, is concerned about the effects this is having on his food choice.

Give him some advice on choosing healthier options for each of the following:

1. a) breakfast
   b) lunch
   c) evening meal

2. Explain how your advice links to the five sections of the eatwell plate.

Activity 2

Working on your own

Look at the following recipes for Pork and Orange Stir Fry with Noodles and Lemon Cheesecake.

Pork and Orange Stir Fry	
Ingredients	**Method**
½ an orange 150 g lean pork steak 1 small clove of garlic 10 ml sunflower oil 75 g red pepper 15 ml salt reduced soy sauce 1.25 ml paprika 1 sheet of noodles	1. Collect the ingredients. 2. Grate the rind from the orange. 3. Peel and segment the orange, keep the juice – add to mug. 4. Cut each segment into two. 5. Crush the garlic. 6. Wash, deseed and dice the red pepper. 7. Wipe the pork and cut into thin strips. 8. Heat the oil and gently fry the garlic. 9. Add the pork and stir fry until lightly coloured but thoroughly cooked. 10. Stir in the pepper and stir fry for 1 minute. 11. Add the rest of the ingredients – soy sauce, paprika, orange and orange juice. 12. Half-fill a pan, add ½ a teaspoon of salt and bring to the boil. Add the noodles and cook for 3 minutes. Drain. 13. Serve the pork on a border of noodles.

Lemon Cheesecake	
Ingredients	**Method**
100 g low fat digestive biscuits – crushed 50 g sunflower margarine 100 g low fat cream cheese 100 ml whipping cream 50 g caster sugar 1 lemon	1. Place flan ring on a paper plate. 2. Crush the biscuits in the food processor. 3. Melt the margarine in a pan, stir in the biscuits. Press mixture firmly into the flan ring and chill. 4. Wash then grate the rind carefully from the lemon. 5. Cut the lemon in half and squeeze the juice. 6. Whip the cream – keep half aside for decoration. 7. Cream the cheese with the sugar, all of the rind and lemon juice then fold in whipped cream. 8. Spread the mixture carefully on top of the crumb base and chill. 9. Carefully remove the flan ring. 10. Decorate by piping theremaining whipped cream and any other appropriate decoration.

1. Describe four ways that current dietary advice has influenced the selection, preparation and use of ingredients.

   Your answers should link to the choice of ingredients, the preparation techniques or methods of cooking.

2. Prepare the dishes. You should:
   a) Select, prepare and/or cook the ingredients according to recipes
   b) Demonstrate specialist garnishing and/or decorating techniques
   c) Work safely and hygienically.

3. If you wish you could take a photo of your finished dishes as evidence.

📁 Portfolio

Do this task well as it could be kept for your portfolio of work.

Activity 3
Work in pairs or in groups

1. Look at a menu from a local food outlet that has not achieved the healthyliving award and highlight any healthy options.

2. Using the information on page 89, make suggestions that would help the food outlet achieve a healthyliving award.

(continued)

Activity 4
Work in pairs or in groups
The school canteen have been asked by the modern languages department to have 'themed days' for each of the following countries.

- Spain
- France
- Germany

The school canteen have got to ensure each of the dishes served promotes healthy eating. You have been set the challenge of designing a healthy dish that is suitable for each of the countries.

If time allows make one of your recipes and get the rest of the class to taste it.

Activity 5
Working on your own
Select a recipe for a main course and dessert.

- Identify three different ingredients that help to meet current dietary advice.
- For each ingredient describe how it meets the current dietary advice.

Rate Your Progress

How confident are you that you have achieved each of the following objectives?

Using the following key as a guide, give yourself a rating for each of the objectives below.

Rating	Explanation
1	Confident with the standard of my work.
2	Fairly confident with the standard of my work.
3	The majority of my work was satisfactory.
4	Require to do some further work.
5	Require a lot of work.

Objectives	Rating
Describe how current dietary advice influences the selection, preparation and use of ingredients.	
Select, prepare and/or cook the ingredients according to recipes.	
Demonstrate specialist garnishing and/or decorating techniques.	
Work safely and hygienically.	

Looking at your ratings

Write down two next steps to 'unlocking' your knowledge of cookery skills, techniques and processes.

4 Get to know your ingredients

By the end of this chapter you should be able to:

- Identify a variety of ingredients from different categories and their characteristics.
- Describe safe and appropriate storage methods for a variety of ingredients.
- Describe how current dietary advice influences the selection, preparation and use of ingredients.
- Describe the importance of sourcing sustainable ingredients.
- Select, prepare and/or cook the ingredients according to recipes.
- Demonstrate specialist garnishing and/or decorating techniques.
- Work safely and hygienically.

NEWS FLASH
The Dietary Goals for Scotland

It is important to use these goals when choosing and using ingredients.

Calories: A reduction in calorie intake by 120kcal/person/day by reducing intake of high fat and/or sugary products and by replacing with starchy carbohydrates (e.g. bread, pasta, rice and potatoes), fruits and vegetables.

Fruit and Vegetables: Average intake of a variety of fruit and vegetables to reach at least 5 portions per person, per day.

Oily Fish: Oil rich fish consumption to increase to one portion (140g) per person, per week.

Red Meat: Average intake of red and processed meat to be around 70g per person, per day.

Fats: Average intake of total fat to reduce to no more than 35% food energy. No more than 11% of this should come from saturated fat i.e. animal fats.

Sugar: Average intake of added sugars to be reduced to less than 11% of food energy in children and adults.

Salt: Average intake of salt to reduce to 6g per day.

Fibre: An increase in average consumption of fibre to increase to 18g per day by increasing consumption of wholegrains, pulses and vegetables.

Topic 1: Meaty matters – meat and meat alternatives

In the UK the main types of meat eaten are beef, veal, lamb, pork and sometimes venison. Many products such as burgers, sausages, meat pies and cook-chill meals can be made from these meats.

Offal is the name for the internal organs of animals, such as liver, kidney and heart.

Meat produced in this country is safe to eat as there are rigorous standards to ensure that the British supply chain is fully traceable from farm to pack. This should encourage consumers to buy more locally produced meats.

> ### 🔍 Hint
> Remember that meat is a good source of protein, iron, and B vitamins, and will usually form the 'core' of a meal.

> ### ❓ Did you know?
> Freedom Food and Red Tractor Symbols on packaging show that meat and poultry have met welfare standards and have been reared with care.

What is meat?

Lean meat is muscle from animals. The muscles are made of cells shaped like long fibres, which are grouped together in bundles. **Invisible fat** is found between bundles of muscle fibres and this fat gives flavour to the meat during cooking. **Visible fat** is found under the skin and is often left on meat joints during cooking to add moisture and flavour.

The texture of all types of meat is affected by . . .

How much **work** the muscles do – tender meat comes from muscles that do little work e.g. loin, rump. Tougher meat comes from muscles that do most work e.g. shin and neck

How it is **cooked** – tougher cuts of meat need to be cooked for longer and usually in liquid to make it tender.
Link Refer back to Chapter 1 Topic 3.

The **age** of the animal – meat from a young animal is more tender.

The flavour of all types of meat is affected by . . .

The **juices** that are squeezed out of the meat as it cooks.

The **fat** in and around the meat.

The method of **cooking** that is chosen, e.g. roasting gives a tasty result.

Current dietary advice and the selection, preparation and use of meat

Hint

Refer to Dietary Goals on page 96.

Selection	Choose lean or extra-lean versions, for example mince and steak for casseroles. Choose cuts of meat that are lean with little visible fat.
Preparation	Trim off visible fat from chops and steak before cooking.
Use	Drain fat off from meat, either after it has been browned or skim off the fat on the surface after it has cooled. Cook brown meats in non-stick pans or use cooking sprays. Choose a method of cookery where no additional fat is added, e.g. stewing, grilling. Mince does not need any additional fat as there is enough invisible fat already through it.

Storage

Meat is a high-risk food, so must be correctly stored to prevent bacteria multiplying. Raw and cooked meats should be stored separately and kept cool in the refrigerator.

Hint

In large-scale kitchens there are separate fridges for raw and cooked produce.

To avoid contaminating other foods, store meat in the bottom of the refrigerator so that no blood can drip onto other foods and cause cross-contamination.

The meat should always be covered – in tinfoil or in a plastic container – and **'use by'** dates should be followed.

Meat alternatives

For some people, e.g. vegetarians who do not eat meat, an alternative source of protein will be used as the 'core' of a meal.

- **Soya beans:** Textured vegetable protein (TVP) is a meat-like product which is made from soya beans. This can be made into different shapes and sizes and even into products that look like ham, beef and poultry. TVP is low in fat and only requires water to make it ready to cook but can be lacking in flavour unless ingredients like chilli, curry powder or tomatoes are added.

  TVP is sometimes added to meat dishes/products to 'bulk' them up and to reduce the cost e.g. burgers

Soya beans

- **Tofu:** This is made by coagulating or setting soya milk and then pressing the resulting curds into soft white blocks. There are many different varieties, including fresh and processed tofu. Tofu can be used in savoury and sweet dishes and is often seasoned or marinated to suit the dish, e.g. for stir fries.

- **Mycoprotein Quorn™:** The Myco protein **Quorn™** is made from a tiny fungus (like a mushroom), which is then fermented, mixed with egg white and flavours then processed. It is easy to use – no preparation is needed and as it only needs reheating it cooks quickly. Mycoprotein can be used for a variety of dishes as it readily absorbs flavours such as curry and tomato. It can be purchased as a fillet, chunks or mince, for use in recipes.

Tofu

✔ Chef's test

Complete the following:

1. Why must meat be stored at the bottom of the refrigerator?
2. How could you reduce the fat content of meat when a) choosing it and b) cooking it?
3. Find out the usual sauces and accompaniments you could serve with the following
   a) Roast beef
   b) Roast lamb
   c) Roast pork
4. Investigate the following:
   • How to store the three different types of meat alternatives.
   • How each one promotes current dietary advice.
5. There are numerous cuts of beef, which can go by different names depending on where you are in the UK. The diagram below shows the various cuts. Select three cuts of meat and for each:
   • List suitable methods of cooking.
   • Find two suitable recipes that could be served in a restaurant.

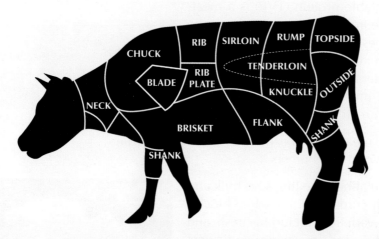

If you want to find out more about cuts of meat go to www.scotchbeefandlamb.com/en/ kitchen-tips/cuts/ where there is information on cuts of beef or lamb. Click on the different cuts of meat to view more information and cooking methods. This website will also give you ideas for recipes for different cuts of meat.

👨‍🍳 Service chef!

Time to make some dishes using meat or meat alternatives.

1. Chilli Con Carne.
2. Spaghetti Bolognese.
3. Lasagne, using minced beef, TVP or Quorn™.
4. Grill Sticks with Tomato Salsa.

Topic 2: The chicken run – poultry and poultry alternatives

Poultry meat comes from birds such as chicken, turkey, ducks and geese. They can be reared in three different ways

Intensively farmed chickens

Free range chickens

- Intensively farmed chickens are reared indoors in confined spaces.
- Free range chickens are allowed outside and are reared in large sheds.
- Organic chicken are allowed to roam free and are fed on organic feed. These are more expensive to buy.

Other types of birds are often served, such as pheasant, partridge and pigeon. These are known as game and are seasonal.

Current dietary advice and the selection, preparation and use of poultry

Selection	Chicken and turkey are generally lower in fat and higher in protein than red meat; goose and duck are more fatty. Try minced chicken or turkey as a lower-fat alternative to minced beef.
Preparation	To reduce fat, remove the skin before cooking or buy skinless chicken/turkey breasts.
Use	When roasting poultry, place the poultry on a rack in the roasting pan so that the fat drips away during cooking. Cooking chicken with the skin on will keep the chicken more moist, but the skin should be removed before eating. Choose a method of cookery where no additional fat is added, e.g. in a stew/casserole or grilling. A selection of vegetables can be added to either of these methods of cookery.

❓ Did you know?

There is white meat and dark meat on chickens and turkeys. White meat is breast meat. Dark meat is found in the wings, thighs, and drumsticks – these parts get more exercise and they have a stronger flavour compared to white meat.

Hint

Remember that frozen poultry should always be thoroughly defrosted before cooking. Check that there are no ice crystals left inside the carcass.

Storage

Raw poultry carries bacteria, such as *Salmonella* and *Campylobacter*, which can pass from one food to another. Poultry should always be covered with foil or clingfilm or sealed in a plastic bag before it is stored at the bottom of the refrigerator, to prevent any of the juices coming into contact with other foods in the fridge.

✔ Chef's test

Complete the following:

1. Why must poultry be stored at the bottom of the refrigerator?

2. How could you reduce the fat content of poultry when a) preparing it and b) cooking it?

3. Find out the usual sauces and accompaniments you could serve with the following:

   a) Roast turkey

   b) Roast duck

   c) Roast goose

4. You have been asked to write an article for a cookery column in the local paper to encourage the use of poultry. You should include the following information:

   • The types of poultry available.

   • How poultry helps meet current dietary advice.

   • How to store poultry safely.

   • One method of cooking that could be used.

   • A recipe that includes this method.

   • Two traditional dishes which use poultry.

   • You can illustrate your article if time allows.

📁 Portfolio

Do this piece of work well as it could be kept for your portfolio of work.

👨‍🍳 Service chef!

Time to make some dishes using poultry and poultry alternatives.

1. Chicken and Potato Flan.

2. Caribbean Chicken.

3. Chicken Biryani.

4. Chicken Lasagne.

Topic 3: A fishy tale – fish and seafood

There are many varieties of fish and seafood, which are caught in seas (saltwater fish) and rivers (fresh water fish) all over the world. To meet demand, fish can also be produced in fish farms, e.g. salmon are kept in netted areas and have their food and health controlled.

Fish are usually grouped into:

- **white fish,** such as haddock, cod, plaice, whiting, coley
- **oily fish**, such as salmon, mackerel, sardines, herring and tuna
- **shellfish**, such as mussels, oysters, prawns, crabs, lobsters, octopus and squid.

Fish can be bought in different ways . . .

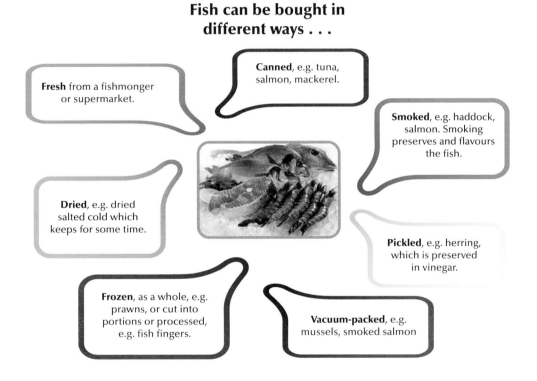

Fresh from a fishmonger or supermarket.

Canned, e.g. tuna, salmon, mackerel.

Smoked, e.g. haddock, salmon. Smoking preserves and flavours the fish.

Dried, e.g. dried salted cold which keeps for some time.

Pickled, e.g. herring, which is preserved in vinegar.

Frozen, as a whole, e.g. prawns, or cut into portions or processed, e.g. fish fingers.

Vacuum-packed, e.g. mussels, smoked salmon

Current dietary advice and the selection, preparation and use of fish

Selection	The flesh of white fish contains less than 5% fat.
	Oily fish contains about 10–20% fat. They are a good source of omega 3 fatty acids, which are important for good heart health and lowering cholesterol.
	The Dietary Goal is to eat one portion of oily fish per week.
	Tuna is only a source of Omega 3 if it is fresh or frozen, not tinned.
Preparation	Coat fish in wholemeal breadcrumbs rather than batter or try cooking 'en papillote' (i.e. in a parcel in the oven).
Use	Fish cooks very quickly so care should be taken not to overcook as it will become tough and dry.
	Choose a method of cookery where no additional fat is added e.g. poaching, grilling, baking or adding fish to a tomato-based sauce.
	Oily fish can be eaten in a variety of ways e.g. sandwiches, pâtés, fillings for baked potatoes, potato topped pies, fish cakes.

❓ Did you know?

The Sea Fish Authority produces a booklet called *The Seafood Guide*. This aims to help chefs, caterers and consumers understand the huge choice of fish and shellfish available in the UK. The guide also includes basic information on preparing seafood, including filleting and portioning whole fish. Tips on storing seafood and what to look out for when buying seafood are also included.

Storage

Fish is very perishable – this means it 'goes off' very quickly. It is best cooked on the day it is bought, but if it has to be stored then rinse it in cold water, dry it and loosely wrap it in foil or cling film before storing in the refrigerator. Store it away from foods such as milk, which will absorb the smell of the fish. Use within 24 hours. Fresh fish can also be frozen if it is not to be cooked on the day it is bought.

☑ Chef's test

Visit the Sea Fish Authority website and the section called 'Nutritionists & teachers' (http://www.seafish.org/nutritionists-and-teachers). Complete the following:

1. What is Omega 3 and why is it good for you?
2. Give two pieces of advice to women on eating fish during pregnancy.
3. Explain two benefits to health of eating fish. You may need to refer to Chapter 3.
4. Describe how you would store a fillet of haddock until it is eaten the next day.

👨‍🍳 Service chef!

Time to make some dishes using fish and seafood.

1. Fish and Cheese Crumble.
2. Smoked Haddock Risotto.
3. Cheesy Tuna Fishcakes.
4. Fish Flan.

Topic 4: From the farm – dairy products and dairy alternatives

Dairy products is the term used to describe food products that are made from milk.

Milk

In the UK, the main source of milk is cows, but other types of milk are available, such as sheep, goats and soya milk. Milk is heat-treated in a variety of ways to destroy bacteria and give it a longer shelf life, and pasteurisation is the most common method.

Chefs will use the following types of milk in different ways depending on the dish they are making.

There are different types of milk

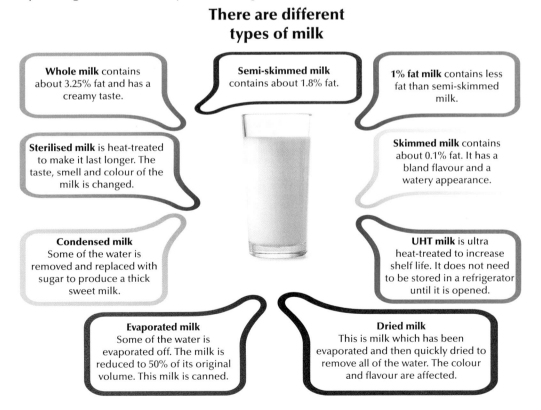

Whole milk contains about 3.25% fat and has a creamy taste.

Semi-skimmed milk contains about 1.8% fat.

1% fat milk contains less fat than semi-skimmed milk.

Sterilised milk is heat-treated to make it last longer. The taste, smell and colour of the milk is changed.

Skimmed milk contains about 0.1% fat. It has a bland flavour and a watery appearance.

Condensed milk Some of the water is removed and replaced with sugar to produce a thick sweet milk.

UHT milk is ultra heat-treated to increase shelf life. It does not need to be stored in a refrigerator until it is opened.

Evaporated milk Some of the water is evaporated off. The milk is reduced to 50% of its original volume. This milk is canned.

Dried milk This is milk which has been evaporated and then quickly dried to remove all of the water. The colour and flavour are affected.

Yoghurt

Yoghurt belongs to a group of products called fermented milks. It is made from warm milk that has had certain types of harmless bacteria added. The yoghurt thickens as the protein sets.

There are many different varieties of yoghurts available including:

- **Low fat yoghurts:** these are made with reduced-fat milk but often have extra sugar added to give them more flavour.
- **Thick-set yoghurts:** these would be used in desserts and soups.
- **Greek or Greek-style yoghurt:** a higher fat version of natural yoghurt with a rich flavour and can be sold premixed with fruit.
- **Bio yoghurts:** these are made with a special type of bacteria that are thought to have a good effect on the digestive system and are often offered as a breakfast choice.

? Did you know?

Fromage frais is made from fermented milk and is in fact a form of soft cheese. Rennet (to set the cheese) and bacteria are added to the milk, which makes it set. It is then stirred until it becomes creamy. Plain fromage frais can be used as an alternative to cream, and lower in fat versions are available.

Cheese

Cheese is made by adding rennet to cow's milk so that the protein in milk coagulates. This forms a curd (a semi-solid substance) which is then pressed to remove the liquid (the whey). The amount of liquid removed will affect the finished texture of the cheese. Salt is added to the curds, which are then packed into moulds and left to ripen for some months or years depending on the type of cheese.

There are different types of cheese

Soft cheese
These cheeses have a soft or creamy texture, e.g. goat's cheese, brie, mozzarella, ricotta.

Semi-hard cheese
These cheeses have a semi-firm but open texture, e.g. gouda, stilton.

Hard cheese
These cheeses have a very firm texture which makes them suitable for grating e.g. cheddar and parmesan.

Processed cheese
A mixture of cheeses, which are grated, melted and poured into moulds. They are sliced or made into different shapes, e.g. triangles.

Unripened cheese
These cheeses are not left to ripen, so usually have a mild flavour, e.g. cottage and cream cheese.

Cooking with cheese

When cheese is gently heated, the cheese melts without losing all the fat. If the heat is too fierce, all the fat runs out, leaving the protein to become tough and hard, which makes it difficult to digest.

Cheese is a very good source of protein and calcium. Most cheese contains about 35% fat. You can buy reduced-fat cheeses but these sometimes do not give the same results when cooked.

Cheese should be mixed with a starchy food like breadcrumbs or potatoes as they absorb the fat, making it easier to digest.

> **? Did you know?**
> Blue veined cheeses like stilton, gorgonzola and Danish blue have a special mould added to the cheese. The mould grows gradually and spreads into the cheese making the blue veins.

Cream

Cream is the fat from milk. Chefs will use different types of cream depending on the dish they are making.

There are different types of cream

Whipping cream
This contains about 35% fat and can be whipped for filling, e.g. choux pastries or as a topping on desserts.

Double cream
This contains 48% fat and whips to a very thick cream that can be used for piping on cakes and desserts.

Single cream
This is slightly thicker than milk and contains about 20% fat. It is used to give richness to some dishes, e.g. curries or soups, and to serve with desserts.

Crème fraîche
This is available in different consistencies and is used as a topping on desserts or added to soups. A low fat version is available.

Clotted cream
This is very thick rich cream and is usually served with scones and jam.

UHT/long-life cream
This is heat-treated and is available as single, double and fat reduced varieties. It has a long shelf life.

Hint

Refer to Dietary Goals for fat, page 96.

Current dietary advice and the selection, preparation and use of dairy products

Selection	Choose reduced-fat versions: • Milk – semi-skimmed, skimmed, 1% milk • Yoghurt – low fat • Cream – whipping • Cheese – e.g. edam, cottage It may be better to use a stronger flavoured cheese and reduce the quantity used, e.g. strong/mature cheddar instead of mild cheddar.
Preparation	Use semi-skimmed or skimmed milk for recipes.
Use	Instead of cream, use reduced-fat fromage frais, crème fraîche or yoghurt as an accompaniment to a dessert, or as a garnish for soup.

Storage

Dairy products must be refrigerated because they are perishable.

Dairy products	Use before the 'use by' date, always check the dates and use the oldest first (stock rotation). Store in a refrigerator on a shelf which is cooler, rather than in the door (industrial fridges do not have door storage).
Milk	Keep milk containers closed and store away from strong-smelling food items in the fridge – the milk can pick up those odours. Whenever possible, leave milk in its original container. Never pour left-over milk back into the original container. Powdered milk should be stored in a cool, dry place but has to be refrigerated once water has been added.
Yoghurt	Once the package is opened, reseal and eat within 3 days. Protect yoghurt from other foods with strong odours by sealing it tightly.
Cheese	The length of time cheese can be kept differs according to the variety; in general, the harder the cheese, the longer it will last. For storage either reseal the cheese in the original package or wrap in clingfilm/tinfoil/plastic food bag and keep in the refrigerator.
Cream	Opened cartons of cream should be resealed and refrigerated immediately after use and used within 3 days.

Hint

Where cheese is to be used as part of a cheeseboard it should be removed from the fridge one hour before serving to allow the flavour to develop.

✔ Chef's test

Complete the following:

1. Name one traditional cheese from each of the following countries:
   a) Holland
   b) France
   c) Italy
   d) Switzerland
   e) Germany
   f) Scotland
2. List two different uses of each of the following types of milk:
   a) UHT
   b) Semi-skimmed
   c) Dried
3. How should you store left-over cheese?
4. Name two different types of cream and give one use for each.
5. Give one health benefit of probiotic yoghurt.

Service chef!

Time to make some dishes using dairy products and dairy alternatives.

1. White Chocolate and Lime Tofu Cheesecake.
2. Spaghetti Carbonara.
3. Smoked Mackerel Pâté with Melba Toast.
4. Pineapple Cream Shortcakes.

Topic 5: Let's get cracking! – eggs

The majority of the eggs eaten in the UK come from hens, although others such as eggs from ducks, geese or quails are also available. Hens eggs are farmed in three ways

- **Eggs from caged birds:** The hens are kept in indoor cages all the time with the temperature, feed and light all controlled.
- **Barn eggs:** Hens are allowed to move about freely inside the building but have no access to the outside.
- **Free range:** The hens are allowed in open-air runs and live in a hen house at night to prevent attack from foxes. Organic eggs are free range and the hens are fed an organic diet. There is an increased demand from consumers for these type of eggs as they are produced with greater consideration for the welfare of the hens and are considered to have a better flavour.

Current dietary advice and the preparation and use of eggs

Preparation	When preparing scrambled eggs in the microwave, no salt needs to be added as the cooking process retains the natural flavour.
	When preparing omelettes, use other ingredients, e.g. herbs, tomato or mushrooms to add flavour rather than salt.
Use	Choose a method of cookery where no additional fat is added, e.g. poaching or boiling.

Cooking with eggs

Eggs have many functions that make them very useful to the chef:

- **Coagulation:** when eggs are heated the protein coagulates or sets and becomes solid.
- **Lightening:** air is trapped, making the product lighter.
- **Emulsification:** helps combinations of some ingredients to mix together and not separate out.

Using eggs in cooking

Coagulation – Binding
When an egg is added to a combination of ingredients, the protein coagulates when heated and binds them together e.g. beefburgers , fishcakes.

Coagulation – Coating
When products, e.g. fishcakes, potato croquettes, are coated in egg and then breadcrumbs, the egg coagulates during cooking and holds the breadcrumbs in place.

Coagulation – Thickening
Egg coagulates on heating gently and so thickens egg sauces, custards, flans, quiches.

Emulsifying
When making mayonnaise the egg yolk prevents the oil from separating from the vinegar.

Lightening
Eggs trap air when whisked or beaten, e.g. meringues, whisked sponges. Egg white traps more air than a whole beaten egg.
Hint: Eggs will trap more air if they are at room temperature when whisked.

Egg allergies

Where consumers have an allergy to eggs, they must take care to read menus carefully and check with the restaurant if eggs have been added into any of the dishes.

Chefs must read food labels carefully to check if eggs have been used in a product as they may be required to answer any queries from the customer.

Storage

- Keep eggs refrigerated after purchase.
- Store eggs blunt end up so that the yolk is surrounded by the white. This helps to keep the egg fresh.
- Store away from strong-smelling food – egg shells are porous allowing any smells to be absorbed.
- Make sure you use eggs by the 'best before' date shown on the egg or box.
- Cooked egg dishes, if not used immediately, should be stored in the refrigerator.
- Never use dirty, cracked or broken eggs.

> **🔍 Hint**
>
> Chefs must be aware of the content of all the products they use, as they may be asked about a range of food allergies, such as nut allergies, or intolerances, e.g. lactose intolerance.

> **🔍 Hint**
>
> Wash your hands before and after handling eggs as there are bacteria on the egg shell.

> **❓ Did you know?**
>
> Look for the Lion Mark on the egg shell and egg box – it shows that the eggs have been produced to the highest standards of food safety. British Lion eggs account for more than 85% of UK egg production.

✔ Chef's test

Complete the following:

1. Explain the following terms:
   a) Coagulation
   b) Lightening
2. Name two dishes that use eggs for each of the following functions.
   a) Coating
   b) Binding
   c) Colour
3. List two points to consider when storing eggs.
4. Hens' eggs are the main type of egg purchased. Name two other types of eggs for sale in the UK.
5. Describe how to prevent a black ring forming around the yolk of a hard-boiled egg.

Service chef!

Time to prepare some dishes using eggs.

1. Nasi Goreng.
2. Lemon Roll.
3. Profiteroles with Chocolate Sauce.
4. Mini Chocolate-Dipped Meringues.
5. Quiche Lorraine.

Topic 6: Take the pledge – fruit and vegetables

If you look in the supermarket you will find that a huge range of fruit and vegetables is available. Some are able to be grown in the UK at certain times of the year when they are in season. Others require a warmer climate and have to be imported from abroad.

For a healthy diet, five portions should be eaten every day and this can be in the form of fresh, frozen, tinned, dried and juices.

Although potatoes are a vegetable, they are not counted as one of the five portions.

Let's look at the more unusual varieties of fruit and vegetables.

Fruit

Melons
There are many varieties of melon e.g. honeydew, water, cantaloupe. The colour of flesh will depend on the variety.

Bananas are sweet with firm and creamy flesh and are available for harvest throughout the year. Bananas are thought to have originated in Malaysia around 4000 years ago. Today, bananas are grown in most tropical and subtropical regions including Costa Rica, Mexico, Ecuador and Brazil.

Kiwi fruit
Originally called a Chinese gooseberry, this fruit was renamed 'kiwi fruit', in honour of the native bird of New Zealand, the kiwi, whose brown fuzzy coat resembled the skin. The green flesh has a fresh tangy flavour and has many small, black, edible seeds. Italy, New Zealand, Chile, France, Japan and the USA are among the leading commercial producers of kiwi fruit.

Mango
This is a tropical fruit with yellow/light orange flesh and a flavour similar to apricots and pineapple. It originates in the Far East.

Figs have green or deep purple skin. They are sweet with a texture that combines the chewiness of their flesh, the smoothness of their skin, and the crunchiness of their seeds. Californian figs are available from June to September; some European varieties are available in autumn.

Physalis
These are also called Cape gooseberries and are small orange fruits. A tropical fruit, its flavour is like a cross between a tomato and a pineapple. It is often used as a garnish.

Citrus fruits
These include lemons, limes, grapefruit, oranges, tangerines and, more unusually, a kumquat, which looks like a small orange. Citrus fruits are valued for the tartness of their juices, their unique fragrances and because they are a good source of vitamin C.

Papayas (also called pawpaws) are pear-shaped fruits. Their flesh is a rich orange-pink colour. Inside the inner cavity of the fruit are black, round seeds encased in a jelly-like substance. The seeds have a peppery bitter flavour so it is not advisable to eat them. They originate in South America.

Pineapples

have a cylindrical shape, a scaly green, brown or yellow skin and a 'crown' of spiny, blue-green leaves and fibrous yellow flesh. Areas that grow pineapples include Hawaii, Thailand, the Philippines, China, Brazil and Mexico.

🔍 Hint

Fruit and vegetables should always be washed before you eat them, as they will have been handled by other people before you bought them.

Vegetables

Peppers
There is a wide range of peppers, e.g. red, green, jalopena, chilli. Most varieties of peppers will turn from green to red and will mellow as they ripen. Care should be taken when preparing chilli peppers not to touch eyes as it will make them sting.

Mangetout
Also called the snow or sugar pea, mangetout are a flat-podded variety of pea, eaten whole while the peas within are still very small – hence the name, which means 'eat everything' in French. Crisp and sweet, they can be served raw, or lightly steamed, boiled or stir-fried.

Pak choi
This leafy green Chinese vegetable belongs to the cabbage family. It has long, green, slightly ribbed leaf stalks and soft, oval, green leaves. The leaves and stems are best suited to brief stir-frying or steaming to retain their mild flavour.

Parsnip
This is root vegetable resembling a carrot but has a cream-coloured flesh. It has a sweet flavour and can be boiled, roasted and baked.

Broccoli is a green vegetable from the cabbage family, originally from Italy. It is generally sold in heads, which have multiple florets branching off a central stem. It is best briefly steamed, stir-fried, or eaten raw. Its colour can range from deep sage to dark green to purplish-green, depending upon the variety.

Aubergine
This can also be called 'eggplant'. They can be bitter so should be salted and rinsed before cooking to remove the bitterness. Aubergines can be baked, stewed, roasted, grilled or fried with a variety of coatings and sauces. Grown in India and Pakistan, they are often used in Mediterranean dishes.

Spinach is a leafy green vegetable that wilts and reduces in volume when cooked. It can also be eaten raw when young enough to be tender. It has a bittersweet taste.

Garlic
This is a strong-smelling member of the onion family which comes originally from Central Asia. Now grown in Europe. Use as a salt substitute, as a flavouring in cooking or on garlic bread. Removing the core from the centre of the garlic helps to prevent the breath smelling of garlic. Washing hands under cold water after handling garlic helps remove the smell from your fingers.

? Did you know?
Garlic contains a substance which scientists say has antibiotic and bactericidal effects. It is believed to promote a healthy heart. It is said that gladiators ate garlic to make them capable of greater feats of strength in the stadium in Roman times.

🔍 Hint
Potatoes are an important source of starch and vitamin C. There are many varieties of potatoes, so it is important to choose the correct type to suit the chosen method of cooking.

Current dietary advice and the selection, preparation and use of fruit and vegetables

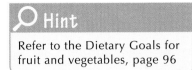

Hint

Refer to the Dietary Goals for fruit and vegetables, page 96

Selection	Buy as fresh as possible.
	Avoid bruised or wrinkled fruit and vegetables.
	Ready prepared produce will have reduced vitamin C due to advance preparation and storage.
	Frozen vegetables will have a higher vitamin C content as they are frozen quickly after being picked.
Preparation	Avoid soaking them, as vitamin C is water soluble and will leach out into the water.
	Do not prepare in advance as vitamin C will be lost through oxidation.
	Knives should be sharp as blunt ones cause more cells to be damaged, resulting in loss of vitamin C.
	Avoid peeling if possible, or peel thinly, as most vitamin C is just under the skin.
	Leave skin on as this will provide more fibre.
Use	Cook vegetables immediately after preparing.
	Add to boiling water and cook for as short a time as possible.
	Use as little water as possible for cooking.
	Choose short methods of cooking, e.g. steaming, microwaving or stir-frying.

Storage

Fruit	Fruit should be kept in a cool, dark place.
	Berries are best kept in the refrigerator.
	Bananas should be kept at room temperature and not in the refrigerator as they will go black.
Vegetables	Remove vegetables from any plastic packaging.
	Leafy vegetables such as spinach, cabbage, cauliflowers etc. should be kept in the refrigerator or cold store.
	Root vegetables like carrots, parsnips, turnip should be kept in a cold store.
	Onions should be kept in a dry, well-ventilated place.
	Potatoes should be kept in racks or in paper bags in a cool, dark, well-ventilated place.
	If kept in the light, potatoes will sprout and turn green, which can be poisonous.

☑ Chef's test

Complete the following:

1. Describe one way of preventing the loss of vitamin C from vegetables when:
   a) Selecting
   b) Preparing
   c) Using

2. You are preparing a fresh fruit salad using pineapple, mango, kiwi fruit and bananas. List one fact about each of these ingredients.

3. What is the nutritional value of fruit and vegetables in our diet?

4. Explain how the following should be stored:
   a) Raspberries
   b) Potatoes
   c) Cabbage

5. Apart from a fresh fruit salad bar, state two other ways a hotel could include more fruit and vegetables in their breakfast menu.

🧑‍🍳 Service chef!

Time to make some dishes using fruit or vegetables.

1. Poached Pears and Raspberry Coullis or Chocolate Sauce.
2. Vegetable Lasagne.
3. Pizza.
4. Raspberry Cream Towers.
5. Apple Flan.

Topic 7: In the store cupboard – dry ingredients

Cereals

Wheat

Wheat is one of the most commonly used cereals throughout the world.

Hint

Refer to the dietary goals for calories on page 96.

Wheat products

Bulgur wheat is a whole wheat grain that has been cracked and partially pre-cooked. It is high in fibre and low in fat. It can be used instead of rice e.g. in a stir fry.

Couscous is made by sprinkling semolina grains with cold salted water and rolling and coating them in fine wheat flour. Couscous can be eaten hot or cold and is a staple ingredient in North Africa.
To prepare couscous stir in boiling water/stock and cover immediately with cling film. Allow the cous cous to swell for 5 minutes before fluffing with a fork to create light fluffy grains

Semolina is a coarse pale-yellow flour ground from hard durum wheat and used to make traditional pasta. It can also be used to make pizza, bread and biscuits. It is also used to make a milk pudding.

Flour

Wheat is usually milled into **flour** and used to make breads, cakes, biscuits and pasta. **Flour** can be purchased in many varieties.

Types of flour

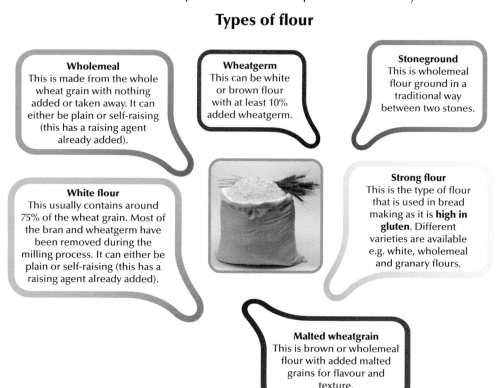

Wholemeal
This is made from the whole wheat grain with nothing added or taken away. It can either be plain or self-raising (this has a raising agent already added).

Wheatgerm
This can be white or brown flour with at least 10% added wheatgerm.

Stoneground
This is wholemeal flour ground in a traditional way between two stones.

White flour
This usually contains around 75% of the wheat grain. Most of the bran and wheatgerm have been removed during the milling process. It can either be plain or self-raising (this has a raising agent already added).

Strong flour
This is the type of flour that is used in bread making as it is **high in gluten**. Different varieties are available e.g. white, wholemeal and granary flours.

Malted wheatgrain
This is brown or wholemeal flour with added malted grains for flavour and texture.

Cooking with flour

Starch and gluten are the two main components of flour.

- **Starch:** In sauce-making, when starch (flour) and liquid are heated, the liquid is absorbed through the walls of the starch granules, which then swell and burst. This thickens the liquid.

- **Gluten** is the protein substance found in strong flour. When the flour is mixed with liquid, the gluten stretches due to the bubbles of gas produced in the dough by the raising agent (yeast), and forms the risen structure of the bread during cooking. Some people are sensitive to **gluten** and develop **coeliac disease**. This is when lining of the intestine is damaged by the gluten and prevents nutrients being absorbed. To cater for those with gluten allergies, there are special flours, breads, baked items and pastas made from gluten-free flour.

Pasta

Pasta is traditionally associated with Italian cuisine, and is a food of ancient origin, which some scholars agree come from the Chinese civilisation and was introduced in Italy by the explorer Marco Polo on his return to Venice.

Pasta is made from durum wheat – a variety of strong flour – which is ground into a fine semolina, The semolina is mixed with water or egg to make a paste. This is then forced through a machine into many different shapes such as penne, spaghetti or sheets of lasagne. The formed dough is then dried under controlled conditions, or left as fresh (undried) pasta.

Watch "how is pasta made" at: http://www.youtube.com/watch?v=kZw5zMqmTdE.

> **? Did you know?**
>
> Eating out can be difficult for people with coeliac disease. A gluten-free restaurant finder at www.glutafin.co.uk will help find a restaurant, bistro, cafe or coffee shop that serves a gluten-free menu.

Storage

Hard dried pasta can be stored in a container for many months. Fresh pasta has to be stored in a refrigerator and used before the shelf life expires.

Other cereals

Oats	Oats used to be the traditional cereal of Scotland, but are now grown throughout the world. Oats are available in different forms. • Oatmeal • Rolled oats • Oat bran and oat germ
Barley	Barley can be grown in Scotland and is available as: • Pearl barley is used to thicken soups, stews. • Barley flour is used for some baking and to thicken soups and stews. • Barley flakes make milk drinks or as a topping for sweet and savoury foods.
Rice	Rice needs wet conditions and is grown in Far Eastern countries such as China. There are many different varieties of rice, each with their own flavour and this includes white, brown and easy cook rice. Rice comes in different forms, such as: • Long grain white/wholegrain used for savoury dishes. • Short grain used for sweet dishes, e.g. rice pudding. • Arborio rice used for risottos.
Rye	Rye can grow in cold climates and is available as: • Rye flour, which can be used to make rye bread or rye biscuits, • Rye grains, which can be added to soups and stews.
Maize	This also known as corn and is available as: • Cornflour, which is maize finely ground into a powder and then used to thicken sauces and stews. • Cornmeal, a flour made from maize which can be used to make pancakes, muffins and polenta (used in Italian cookery).
Spelt	• Spelt is a cereal grain in the wheat family. The grain has been cultivated for centuries, in both central Europe and the Middle East. It looks very similar to wheat in appearance, but it has a much harder outer shell before it is milled. It has a nutty and slightly sweet flavour, similar to that of whole wheat flour. The flour is pale greyish-yellow, gritty, and has a sweetish, nutty flavour. • Spelt doesn't always have to be ground into flour. The grains can also be cooked and added to side dishes, salads and cereals.

Storage

All types of cereal should be stored, covered, in a cool and dry area. This prevents them from absorbing moisture and smells and from attracting insects, such as flour or rice weevils, or rodents. It is better not to mix new flour with old if you are not using the flour regularly.

Breakfast cereals

Many cereals are made into breakfast cereals. Breakfast cereals can be a healthy start to the day as they are usually fortified with a range of minerals such as iron, and vitamins such as the B group and D. Breakfast cereals can also be a good source of fibre.

Store breakfast cereals in an airtight container, so they do not absorb moisture and become soft.

Current dietary advice and the selection, preparation and use of cereals

Current advice is to eat more total complex carbohydrates, such as bread and especially wholemeal and brown breads, breakfast cereals and pasta.

Selection	• Wholemeal varieties of cereal products will provide more fibre in the diet and be more filling. • Read the nutritional information on cereal products such as breakfast cereals and bread mixes carefully as they may contain more sugar, fat or salt than you think.
Preparation	• Pasta is sometimes considered a fattening food, but it is the sauces and additional ingredients used in the pasta that makes it a heavy food. Serve with a tomato-based sauce rather than a cream-based sauce and include a variety of vegetables. • Pastry and other baked products can be prepared using a mix of white and wholemeal flours.
Use	• Wholemeal flour can be used to thicken sauces. • Use wholemeal varieties of bread in desserts e.g. bread pudding, summer pudding, sandwiches, toasties. • Breakfast cereals such as oats can be used as toppings on puddings.

Sugar

Sugar is extracted from sugar cane or beet and a black syrup called molasses is left over. In white sugar, all of the molasses has been removed but in brown sugar some of the molasses remains.

There are many different types of sugar. They are identified by the size of the sugar crystal and the colour.

Sugar

Granulated sugar is white. It is a general all-purpose sugar used to sweeten e.g. in hot drinks, and stewed fruit.

Soft light brown sugar: Small crystals of refined white sugar treated with light-coloured molasses.

Dark brown sugar: Small crystals of refined white sugar treated with dark coloured molasses. All brown sugars will give cakes and biscuits a darker colour and is traditionally used in rich fruit cakes.

Icing sugar: This is made from granulated sugar that is pulverised to a very fine white powder. The crystals are very small. It can be used for icings and sprinkled for decoration.

Caster sugar is specially milled and sifted to make finer crystals that are cube-shaped. It is used for creaming cakes, whisked sponges and meringues.

Preserving sugar: These crystals are larger than granulated sugar and are used in jam making.

Demerara sugar: These crystals are larger and coarser than granulated and are pale brown in colour. Demerara sugar can be sprinkled on top of a dessert, e.g. crème brulée, which can then be grilled to give a crisp topping.

Storage

Sugar becomes damp very easily so all types should be kept in an airtight container in a dry place

Brown sugar can become very hard and dry if not stored correctly. If this happens, place it in a bowl, cover with a damp cloth, and leave until it becomes soft and easily broken up.

Current dietary advice and the selection, preparation and use of sugars

A diet that is high in sugar is unhealthy. The average intake of added sugars should be less than 11% of food energy in children and adults.

> 🔍 **Hint**
> Refer to the Dietary Goals for sugar, page 96.

Selection	• Read food labels before selecting foods to see the sugar content. Remember that ingredients ending in 'ose' are usually sugars, e.g. sucrose, fructose etc.
Preparation	• Replace some sugar in recipes with dried fruit such as sultanas.
Use	• Sugar alternatives could be used to replace sugar in some recipes, e.g. in stewed fruit. Although they can be used in baking they may not give similar results.

? Did you know?

Some dried beans like kidney beans contain toxins in their outer skin so must be soaked for 12 hours and then boiled for 15 minutes to destroy these toxins. Canned beans are safe to use as they have already been heat-treated.

There are many varieties of tinned beans, some of which come in a sauce, such as kidney beans in a chilli sauce.

Pulses

Pulses are the seeds of plants and include beans, lentils and peas. Many can be dried, such as lentils and many varieties of beans, for example kidney, soya, aduki, black eyed, haricot, cannellini and chickpeas.

Pulses should be stored in an airtight container.

Current dietary advice and the use of pulses

Use	• Pulses are good sources of protein and fibre. They also provide carbohydrates, vitamin B complex and iron.
	• Add pulses to a dish to increase the protein content, e.g. add kidney beans to a chilli, or to reduce the meat content.

✔ Chef's test

Complete the following:

1. Name at least six varieties of pasta.
2. Give a brief description of how pasta is made.
3. State one use of each of the following types of sugar:
   a) Demerara
   b) Icing
   c) Granulated
   d) Caster

   What is gluten and how is it affected during cooking?
4. Name the group of people who are allergic to gluten.
5. Which breakfast cereals are the best choice and explain why.
6. Explain the term 'fortification' and give two examples of foods that are fortified.

👨‍🍳 Service chef!

Time to make some dishes using dry ingredients.

1. Mediterranean Couscous.
2. Macaroni and Beef Bake.
3. Lentil and Tomato Soup.
4. Mini Lemon Bakewell Tarts.

Topic 8: Spice it up! – herbs, spices, flavourings, seasonings

Herbs

Herbs are natural occurring flavours for use in foods. They can be either fresh or dried. As the water has been removed from dried herbs they have a stronger more concentrated flavour, so less is used in dishes.

Bay leaf • Bay leaves come from the sweet bay or laurel tree. If eaten whole, they have a sharp, bitter taste. They are usually sold dried. • Bay leaves can be used to flavour vinegars and pâtés, and in pickling and marinades. Long cooking draws out the aroma of this herb and most braised, poached and stewed dishes benefit from the addition of a bay leaf, as do soups, stocks and risottos. The bay leaf should be removed before serving.	**Basil** • Basil grows well in warm climates and is widely used throughout southern Europe, particularly the Mediterranean, and in many parts of Asia. • The leaves have a sweet aromatic smell. Fresh basil leaves are used as garnishing. Dried and crushed the leaves are used mainly in Italian tomato sauces, giving a sweet scented, minty aroma. • Purple basil is good for enhancing salads.
Coriander • Most of the commercially produced coriander is grown in Morocco, Romania and Egypt. • Coriander is the name given to the seeds of the plant while the leaves are known as Cilantro. The leaves are bright green and are added to or sprinkled over spicy food. • Coriander is an important ingredient in curries. The seeds are used whole (in stews) or ground in both savoury and sweet foods. Both have a citrus flavour. 	**Chives** • The smallest member of the onion family, chives are a popular herb used in European cookery. • They have long, thin, green blades that are hollow inside. They have a mild, grassy flavour similar to baby spring onions or young leeks. • They can be chopped or snipped and added to salads, rice, omelettes and pasta dishes. 
Dill • Dill is native to southern Russia, western Africa and the Mediterranean region. • The seeds are stronger and have more flavour than the leaves and are associated with the cuisines of Scandinavia and Germany. • Its green leaves have a soft, sweet taste and are used with many fish dishes, e.g. salmon.	**Marjoram** • This culinary herb is from the same family as oregano. There are several varieties of marjoram; all have different-sized leaves that are green, yellow or variegated. Although all marjoram varieties are fragrant and taste delicate when cooked, each has a different flavour depending on the climate in which it has been grown. • It goes well with potatoes, eggs and tomatoes and can be added to beef stews.

(continued)

Mint

- There are many different species of mint, but the one used most widely in Western cooking is spearmint, native to the Mediterranean and widely grown in the UK.
- It can be made into mint sauce or jelly as an accompaniment to roast lamb. Mint leaves can be added to the water used to boil new potatoes and peas.

Oregano

- This popular herb whose name means 'mountain joy' is available throughout the year. It can be found growing wild on mountainsides in Greece and other Mediterranean countries as well in the UK.
- Oregano has a strong smell and a slightly bitter, spicy taste.
- Oregano is most commonly used as a seasoning in stews, pizzas and tomato-based sauces. Fresh oregano leaves can enhance the flavour of salads and soups as well as Mediterranean and Mexican dishes.

Parsley

- It was not until the Romans came along that parsley started to be cultivated as a garnish. It is now cultivated all over the world and is frequently used as a garnish.
- The two most popular types of parsley are curly parsley and Italian flat leaf parsley. The Italian variety has a more fragrant and stronger taste than the curly variety and tends to be preferred in Mediterranean cooking.

Rosemary

- Although rosemary is native to the Mediterranean, it now grows throughout much of the temperate regions in Europe and America.
- The taste and colour of rosemary comes from the oil within the leaves. It has a woody, pine like flavour with a hint of lemon and is used to flavour chicken, lamb, pork, salmon and tuna dishes as well as many soups and sauces.

Tarragon

- Often used in French cooking, this herb has long, soft green leaves and a distinctive aniseed flavour. It goes well with fish and chicken and can also be used to flavour oils and vinegars.
- Dried tarragon retains much of the flavour of fresh, which is useful if fresh is not available. It is one of the herbs that make up 'fines herbes'.

Thyme

- This is a member of the mint family and has a minty, lemony flavour. The leaves are very small and are easily chopped. They are added to stuffings along with parsley.

? Did you know?

Did you know that the Romans brought mint to Britain, and used it as a mouth freshener and an aid to digestion.

Spices

Spices are the dried flowers, seeds, leaves, bark and roots of fragrant plants. Most spices are available whole or ground into a powder. Spices are not only a great flavouring on their own, but can also act as a preservative and flavour-enhancer for particular ingredients.

Allspice	Cardamom
• This is the dried fruit of the pimento tree. It is called allspice because it tastes like a mixture of nutmeg, cloves and cinnamon. • It is used in baking, pickling and as flavouring in some meat dishes such as pork stir fry. 	• The cardamom plant is native to India and Sri Lanka and is also grown in Guatemala, Mexico, Indonesia and other areas of southern Asia. • Ground cardamom seeds can be used to flavour curries, soups, pâtés, stews, purées and rice dishes. It can also be used in sweet dishes such as ice cream, custard, breads and pastries or sprinkled over a fresh fruit salad.
Cayenne pepper	**Cinnamon**
• This is made by grinding the pod and seeds of dried chilli peppers that came originally from Cayenne in South Africa. • It is a bright red/orange colour and is very 'hot', so must be used in small amounts, e.g. in curries. 	• Cinnamon has a sweet, woody fragrance and was originally grown in Sri Lanka. • The spice is obtained from the inner bark of the cinnamon tree. The bark is stripped from the tree and allowed to dry in the sun. While drying, it is rolled up into a cinnamon stick. Some of the quills are then ground down into a powdered cinnamon. • Ground cinnamon is commonly used in baking. The cinnamon sticks are used for flavouring pilaus, biryanis and meat dishes but are removed before serving.
Cloves	**Cumin**
• These are dried flower buds of the clove tree. Cloves are strong, pungent and sweet. • Cloves are used in many meat dishes, marinades, pickles and in baking, either whole or in powder form. 	• The cumin is native to the Mediterranean and Egypt. Nowadays, it is grown in Iran, Turkey and Syria, and other hot countries as far as China and India. • Cumin is a main component of curry powder and a number of hot spice mixtures including 'garam masala'. • Cumin has a strong, savoury taste. It is a popular spice, particularly in Mexican, North African and Indian cuisines.

(continued)

Ginger	Chilli powder
• This is the root of a plant grown in south-east Asia. • It is available fresh as root ginger or dried as ground ginger. Fresh ginger has a strong 'hot' taste and is used in stir fry and curries. Ground ginger is used in baking, e.g. gingerbread. • Fresh unpeeled ginger root, tightly wrapped, can be refrigerated for up to 3 weeks and frozen for up to 6 months.	• Chilli powder is a blend of ground chillis and other spices and herbs. Ingredients in chilli powder can include cayenne pepper, paprika, cumin, oregano, garlic powder and salt. • Chilli powder is not the same as cayenne pepper. Pure cayenne pepper is much hotter than chilli powder.
Paprika	**Garam masala**
• Paprika is a spice that comes from a type of sweet red pepper or paprika peppers which are produced in Spain, California and Hungary. Hungarian paprika is famed throughout the world for its flavour and quality. • The seeds are removed from the fruit and the peppers are then dried and subsequently ground down into a deep red powder. The powder varies in taste from mildly hot to mildly sweet. It is used in Hungarian cookery to make goulash, the national dish. It goes well with meat, chicken and fish.	• An aromatic mixture of ground spices used as a base in many Indian dishes ('masala' means spice). • The proportion of spices changes according to the dish being cooked but usually includes coriander, cardamom, cinnamon, cloves and black pepper, depending on whether the dish includes meat, vegetables or fish.
Turmeric	**Curry powder/paste**
• Turmeric is made from the dried root of the turmeric plant. It is usually bought in a dried, powdered form. • It has a very intense, bright yellow-orange colour and spicy taste. It is used as an ingredient in curry powder and in pickles, curries and rice dishes. • Turmeric can stain work surfaces so care should be taken when using it.	• Up to 20 spices – including coriander, cumin, and turmeric – can make up a curry powder or paste.

❓ Did you know?

Mono sodium glutamate (MSG), is made from sugar beets and wheat protein and is often added to Chinese food as a flavouring. Some people are allergic to MSG. Additional care must be taken with products containing it, as they will be high in salt.

Flavourings

The most common type of flavourings used are extracts and oils, which are concentrated flavours from a variety of sources. They add both taste and aroma.

- **Extracts** are concentrated flavourings diluted by an alcohol or water base. They are good standbys to use for baking. Extracts such as vanilla or peppermint are much stronger than essences of the same flavours, so less is required.

- **Oils** work much in the same way as extracts, except they are more highly concentrated. They are usually considered to be 3–4 times stronger than extracts. As oils are so concentrated, you will only need a small amount compared to using an extract when baking. Examples include banana, strawberry and peach oils.

- **Flavoured cooking oil** can be purchased for use in stir fries but it is cheaper to make your own by adding herbs – dried or fresh - or spices to a good-quality oil. For example: garlic, basil or chilli.

Seasonings

The two most common seasonings used are salt and pepper.

🔍 Hint

Refer to Dietary Goals for salt, page 96.

Table salt	Rock salt
• Table salt, the one found in most salt shakers, is mined from salt deposits and has most of the minerals removed. • Table salt is made by driving water into a salt deposit (in a mine). This process forms a brine, which is then evaporated, leaving dried cube-like crystals that look like granulated sugar. Most table salts contain additives such as anticaking agents.	• Rock salt is a coarse version of the finely ground table salt. Its coarse texture makes it easy to pick up and sprinkle on food during or after cooking. • It can also be used in a salt mill. • Rock salt is very often used in the brine of tinned foods.
Sea salt	**Salt substitutes**
• Produced from evaporating salt water collected from an ocean or sea. The process is more costly than the mining process. • Sea salt is less refined than other salts. • Depending on the seawater used, there is also a variety of minerals in the sea salt but only in very small amounts. Chefs believe that sea salt has a better texture and flavour than ordinary table salt. It can be used in a salt mill.	• These are available for people on low-salt diets. • They contain little or no sodium and are normally made of potassium chloride. It is the sodium content that contributes to high blood pressure, which can increase the risk of heart disease and stroke.

Some of the major producers of pepper nowadays are India, Indonesia, Vietnam, Brazil, Malaysia, Sri Lanka, Thailand and China.

Pepper	
Black pepper	**White pepper**
• This is produced from the still-green unripe berries of the pepper plant. The berries are cooked briefly in hot water, both to clean them and to prepare them for drying. The heat ruptures cell walls in the fruit, speeding the work of browning enzymes during drying. The berries are dried in the sun or by machine for several days, during which the fruit around the seed shrinks and darkens into a thin, wrinkled black layer. Once dried, the fruits are called black peppercorns, which are then ground into black pepper. • Black pepper is the most important and popular spice in the world. It can be added to almost every savoury dish, hot or cold, giving a sharp and strong flavour.	• This consists of the seed only, with the skin of the fruit removed. This is usually done by a process known as "retting" where fully ripe berries are soaked in water for about a week, during which the flesh of the fruit softens and decomposes. Rubbing then removes what remains of the fruit and the seed that is left is then dried. • Generally, white pepper is not as strong as black. It is preferred by chefs for, light-coloured sauces or mashed potatoes, where black pepper would show as black specks.

❓ Did you know?
- For health reasons, some people are advised to reduce their intake of salt.
- It is not healthy to have more than 6g per day. Substituting salt with a range of herbs and spices is a much healthier way of cooking and eating. Research is now proving that certain spices can actually prevent cardiovascular disease, including strokes and heart attacks.

❓ Did you know?
Supermarkets sell mixed peppercorns, which can be ground in a pepper mill and can be used in the same way as black pepper. They offer different flavours, depending on the peppercorns used.

Storage

Current dietary advice and the selection and use of herbs, spices, flavourings and seasonings

Use a range of these to make the dish more healthy and to reduce salt and sugar content.

Herbs	**Fresh growing herbs** should be kept in a cool place and the soil should be kept moist. Many supermarkets sell **pre-cut fresh herbs** in sealed bags which require refrigeration after purchase. Buying bags of **pre-cut herbs** may be more cost effective for large catering establishments as they will be used quickly and not require long storage. **Dried herbs** should be stored in an airtight container.
Spices	Always store spices in an airtight container and place them in a dark area such as a cupboard. A spice rack above the cooker may look good, however, spices should be kept away from moisture, sunlight and sources of heat, all of which damage the spices.
Flavourings	Store in the original bottle and use before the best before date to prevent loss of flavour.
Seasonings	Salt is often stored in the container in which it is bought. It can also be stored in an airtight container so the salt does not become moist.

Hint

It is best to buy all dried herbs and spices in small quantities and use by the 'best before' date so that they retain their aroma and flavour. It is important that the containers are properly resealed after use.

Hint

Be careful in the use of ready-made mixed seasonings as many of these include a lot of salt.

Chef's test

Complete the following:

1. State two ways of purchasing herbs and describe how each should be stored.
2. What is MSG and what are the health concerns about its use?
3. Describe the three different types of pepper and their uses.
4. Give three points when storing spices to ensure the flavour is retained.
5. Describe the difference between rock salt and sea salt.

Service chef!

Time to make some dishes using herbs, spices, flavourings, seasonings.

1. Spicy Chicken and Apricot stew with Couscous.
2. Stir Fried Pork with Noodles.
3. Spiced Leek and Potato Soup.
4. Pasta with a Tomato and Basil Sauce.

Topic 9: Sustainable food

The word **sustainable** means 'being able to maintain or keep something going for a length of time'.

In food terms, sustainability takes into account the process from field to plate. It is about finding ways of providing foods that are accessible throughout the year and have less of an impact on the environment. Chefs have to consider sustainability when deciding on menus to ensure the required ingredients are continually available.

The ABC of key words that are linked to sustainability

- **Carbon footprint**: Your **carbon footprint**, associated with the food you eat, is the **greenhouse gas** emissions produced by growing, rearing, farming, processing, transporting, storing, cooking and serving the food on your plate. Increasing concern over carbon emissions has led to the growth of the number of consumers who would prefer to eat only 'locally' grown food and know its origin. For this reason many restaurants will use 'locally grown produce' as a promotional feature.

- **Economics**: Home grown food often comes without the costs of processing, packaging and distribution. Also, the more we grow, the less we need to buy, the lower our carbon footprint should be. Food that's grown in season does not need to be grown in heated greenhouses. So it takes less energy and costs less to produce. Food producers may pass on these savings to consumers in the form of lower prices.

- **Environmental impact**: Food and drink processors and retailers in Scotland should be encouraged to help the environment by:
    - reducing packaging that contributes to waste
    - recycling packaging
    - increasing transport efficiencies – food transportation over long distances adds to carbon dioxide emissions, which in turn contribute to climate change
    - include more Scottish seasonal produce when it is available
    - support 'fair trade' efforts for Scottish farmers as well as international farmers
    - source produce within Scotland. This would help reduce **food miles**.

- **Food miles:** This is the distance that food travels from 'field to fork' – the journey from where food is grown or produced

to the consumer. Food miles make us aware of the effect on the environment of transporting food around the world.

- **Locality:** Consumers and catering suppliers may have the option of buying from farmers' markets or buying food direct from local food producers.
  - This type of shopping means buying direct and is a good way to buy foods in season at their freshest, and possibly save money.
  - Farmers' markets will often have samples of local produce to taste.
  - Many chefs use this opportunity to demonstrate how they use local produce on their menus.
  - Buying produce direct from a farm should also mean tastier and fresher produce. Farm produce boxes contain a selection of in season vegetables, fruit, meat, and fresh eggs to order.
  - Some farms will offer organic produce.
  - Because a farm produce box is delivered direct to the door of a restaurant, this can help to cut down on shopping trips, saves time and fuel emissions, helping to create a cleaner environment.
  - Fresh fruit and vegetables do not come wrapped in plastic when bought from a farm. So buying a farm produce box also helps to reduce packaging waste and pollution.
  - Some of the bigger hotels are developing their own gardens to grow fresh fruits, herbs and vegetables for the chefs to use.
- **Seasonality:** Seasonal food refers to the time of year when food is at its best for flavour and is grown in the country that offers the best climate for its production e.g. soft fruit in Scotland, rice in India.
  - In today's global food market most foods are available all year round but when local, seasonal food is available it tends to be fresher and cheaper because there has been less transportation and storage time from farm to fork. Eating seasonal food tends to be tastier, healthier and better for the environment.
  - Eating according to the seasons has disappeared for most people in the developed world. You can buy asparagus and strawberries all year round thanks to refrigeration, heated greenhouses and global food transportation.

– Eating local food according to the seasons is the most sustainable option and is being encouraged by various initiatives throughout the country.

– Chefs are using more seasonal foods on their menu by offering a 'Specials' menu in addition to their regular menu.

✔ Chef's test

Complete the following:

1. Go to http://www.greenerscotland.org/eating-greener/eating-in-season-food and download the **In Season Food Calendar**. Choose a season.

   a) Identify three vegetables, two fruits, three meats and three fish in season at that time of year.

   b) Suggest three recipes that include these ingredients.

2. What is sustainable food and how is it important to chefs?

3. Describe two advantages of buying locally produced food.

4. Explain the term 'food miles' and its impact on the environment.

🍳 Service chef!

The In Season Food Calendar for the month of October shows the following vegetables are in season. Make a soup or vegetarian main course using at least three of them to show the use of seasonal vegetables.

beetroot, broccoli, brussels sprouts, butternut squash, cabbage, carrots, cauliflower, celeriac, celery, courgettes, fennel, kale, leeks, lettuce, mushrooms, onions, parsnips, potatoes, pumpkin, runner beans

GO! End of chapter activities

Activity 1

Working on your own

Choose at least **eight** ingredients from the two recipes below.

1. Place each ingredient in the correct category in the following table.

2. Give one characteristic of each ingredient – this could include reference to the origin of the ingredient, a link to a traditional dish made using the ingredient or the taste of the ingredient.

(*continued*)

Macaroni and Beef Bake	Lemon Roll
Ingredients	**Ingredients**
125 g minced beef	75 g plain flour
50 g onion	3 medium eggs
1 clove of garlic	75 g caster sugar
75 ml beef stock	25 g butter
150 ml chopped tomatoes	150 ml whipping/double cream
25 g mushrooms	75 g cream cheese
25 g red or green pepper	15 ml icing sugar
2.5 ml mixed herbs	10 ml lemon curd
1 bay leaf	Juice and rind of half a lemon
salt and pepper	
75 g macaroni	
30 g grated parmesan cheese	

Category	Ingredient	Characteristic
Meat and meat alternatives		
Poultry and poultry alternatives		
Fish and seafood		
Dairy products and dairy alternatives		
Eggs		
Fruit and vegetables		
Dry ingredients		
Herbs, spices, flavourings, seasonings		

Activity 2

Working in a group or as a class

Produce a wall display to show three types of fish – white, oily and shellfish. It should include:

- pictures of the three types of fish.
- sources

 Portfolio

Do this task well as it could be kept for your portfolio of work.

- how to cook
- how to garnish
- traditional fish dishes of different countries

Activity 3

Working on your own
Investigate each of the following ingredients:
- Fromage frais
- Greek yoghurt
- Probiotic yoghurt
- Crème fraîche

1. Give a description of each of the products – the origin, production and use in cooking.
2. Find a recipe using each of the ingredients.
3. If time allows, make one of the recipes.

Activity 4

Working on your own
Look at the following recipe for a meat pie with a mashed potato topping.

Topping	Method
Topping 200 g potatoes 25 ml milk 15 g butter **Base** 250 g minced meat 50 g chopped onion 5 ml oil 25 g flour 125 ml stock seasoning	1. Wash and peel the potatoes. Cut into large, even sized pieces and add to water and boil for 15–20 minutes, until soft. Drain, dry off and mash, adding the butter and milk. 2. Put on the oven at Gas Mark 5, 195°C. Heat the oil, sauté the onions for 2 minutes, add the mince and brown, stir in the flour and cook for about 1 minute. Add the stock, boil then simmer for 15 minutes. Taste for seasoning. 3. Place the mince mixture in the bottom of a dish, carefully spread the potatoes over the mince and bake for 15 minutes until golden-brown.

a) Identify at least four changes that could be made to this recipe to make it link better to current dietary advice. This could include changes to the ingredients, preparation techniques or cooking methods. Present your information in a table.

Changes	Describe why these make the recipe better

(continued)

Look at each of the four ingredients from the recipe in the table below.

b)

- Describe how each should be prepared for storage.
- State where it should be stored.

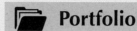

Portfolio

Do this piece of work well as it could be kept for your portfolio of work.

Ingredient	Preparation for storage	Storage
Flour		
Potatoes		
Minced meat		
Milk		

Activity 5

Working on your own

Make up a crossword or a wordsearch using the information in this topic. You can create a crossword by going to www.eclipsecrossword.com and following the instructions.

Activity 6

Working on your own

As a **chef** in a local hotel, you have been asked to provide two dishes for a meal that represents the best of Scottish produce. You have decided to make Fish Flan and Raspberry Cream Towers.

Fish Flan

Ingredients

Pastry	Filling
50 g plain flour	75 g fresh fish e.g. salmon, smoked haddock, white fish
50 g oatmeal	50 ml semi-skimmed milk
50 g margarine	1 egg
15–30 ml water	30 g grated mature cheddar cheese
Equipment:1 15cm flan ring	5 ml finely chopped chives
	seasoning

Method

1. Heat oven to Gas Mark 6 or 200°C.
2. Place flour and oatmeal in a baking bowl. Rub in margarine.
3. Mix with water until a stiff paste is formed.
4. Knead the pastry on a lightly floured surface. Roll out the pastry and use it to line the flan ring.
5. Chill in the fridge for 10 minutes. Trim and bake blind for 10 minutes.
6. Mix the egg, milk and 2/3 of the cheese together. Lightly season.
7. Reduce the oven temperature to Gas Mark 5 or 190°C.
8. Cut up the fish into small cubes and place in the pastry case. Pour the egg mixture over. Sprinkle the remaining cheese on top.
9. Bake for 20–25 minutes until set.
10. Garnish appropriately before serving.

Raspberry Cream Towers

Ingredients

75 g plain flour

3 eggs

75 g caster sugar

40 g grated white chocolate or toasted coconut

250 ml whipping cream

50 g raspberries

Method

1. Heat oven to Gas Mark 6, 200°C.
2. Grease and line a 20×30cm baking tray.
3. Put the eggs and caster sugar into a glass baking bowl and whisk until thick and creamy (when it leaves a trail in the mixture).
4. Sieve the flour on to the top of the egg mixture and carefully fold in using a figure of eight.
5. Pour into the baking tray and gently tilt to cover the tray evenly.
6. Bake in the oven for 8–10 minutes until golden-brown and well risen. Lightly touch the centre of the sponge and it should be springy.
7. Place a piece of grease-proof paper on to the surface and lightly sprinkle with caster sugar.
8. Turn the sponge out on to the sugared paper and leave until cooled.
9. Place the chocolate or toasted coconut on a large plate.
10. Whisk the cream until soft peak consistency.
11. Place half of the cream into a small bowl and mix in the raspberries carefully.
12. Cut the sponge into 8×7.5 cm circles.
13. Sandwich the sponges together to make four individual towers.
14. Spread a little of the remaining cream thinly round the sides of the towers and coat with the grated chocolate or toasted coconut.
15. Spread a little of the cream on top of each tower.
16. Finish each tower with piped cream, serve on a small plate and decorate appropriately.

Stage 1. Prepare the dishes.
- a) Select, prepare and/or cook the ingredients according to recipes.
- b) Demonstrate specialist garnishing and/or decorating techniques.
- c) Work safely and hygienically.
- d) If you wish, you could take a photo of your finished dishes as evidence.

Stage 2. Choose eight ingredients from your two recipes:
- a) Place each ingredient in the correct category in the given table (complete at least five different categories).
- b) Give one characteristic of the ingredient — this could include reference to the origin of the ingredient, a link to a traditional dish made using the ingredient or the taste of the ingredient.

(continued)

Category	Ingredient	Characteristic
Meat and meat alternatives		
Poultry and poultry alternatives		
Fish and seafood		
Dairy products and dairy alternatives		
Eggs		
Fruit and vegetables		
Dry ingredients		
Herbs, spices, flavourings, seasonings		

Stage 3. Select four ingredients you identified above; each one should come from a different category.

    a) Describe how it should be prepared for storage.

    b) State where you should store it.

Ingredient	Preparation for storage	Storage place

Stage 4. Referring to the two recipes you have selected, describe **four ways** in which current dietary advice has influenced any of the following:

- selection of the ingredients **or**
- choice of preparation techniques **or**
- cooking techniques.

Stage 5. Describe the importance of sustainability. Your description should include reference to at least one implication of sustainability from the following list, linked to the ingredients in your dish:

- carbon footprint
- environmental impact
- locality
- seasonality
- economics.

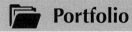 **Portfolio**

Do this task well as it could be kept for your portfolio of work.

Rate Your Progress

How confident are you that you have achieved each of the following objectives?

Using the following key as a guide, give yourself a rating for each of the objectives below.

Rating	Explanation
1	Confident with the standard of my work.
2	Fairly confident with the standard of my work.
3	The majority of my work was satisfactory.
4	Require to do some further work.
5	Require a lot of work.

Objectives	Rating
Identify a variety of ingredients from different categories and their characteristics.	
Describe safe and appropriate storage methods for a variety of ingredients.	
Demonstrate specialist garnishing and/or decorating techniques.	
Describe how current dietary advice influences the selection, preparation and use of ingredients.	
Describe the importance of sourcing sustainable ingredients.	
Select, prepare and/or cook the ingredients according to recipes.	
Work safely and hygienically.	

Looking at your ratings

Write down two next steps to 'unlocking' your knowledge of understanding and using ingredients.

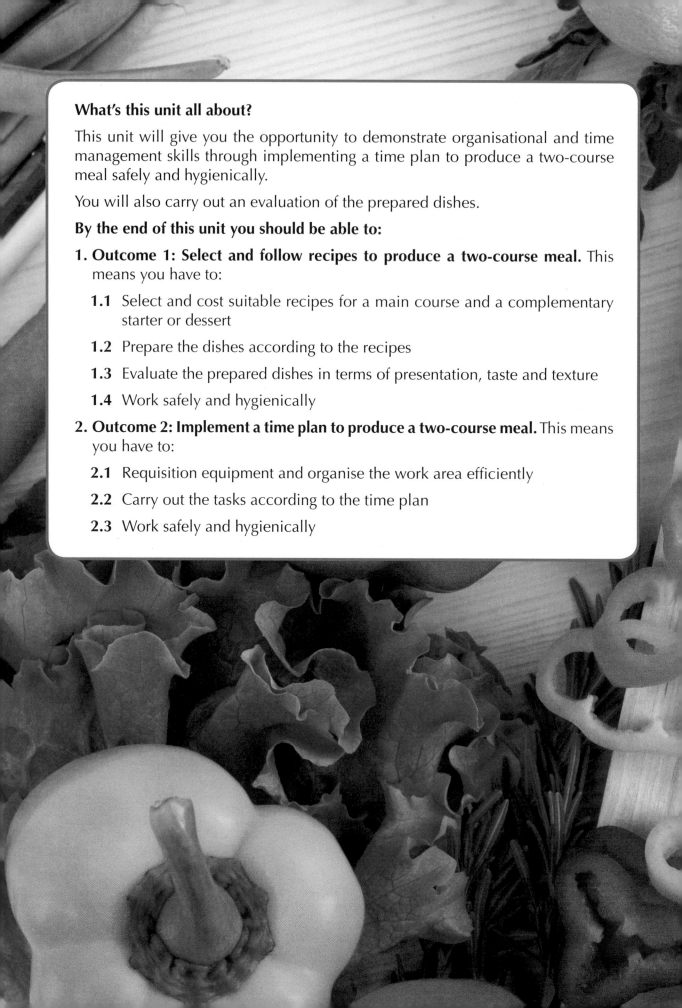

What's this unit all about?

This unit will give you the opportunity to demonstrate organisational and time management skills through implementing a time plan to produce a two-course meal safely and hygienically.

You will also carry out an evaluation of the prepared dishes.

By the end of this unit you should be able to:

1. **Outcome 1: Select and follow recipes to produce a two-course meal.** This means you have to:

   1.1 Select and cost suitable recipes for a main course and a complementary starter or dessert

   1.2 Prepare the dishes according to the recipes

   1.3 Evaluate the prepared dishes in terms of presentation, taste and texture

   1.4 Work safely and hygienically

2. **Outcome 2: Implement a time plan to produce a two-course meal.** This means you have to:

   2.1 Requisition equipment and organise the work area efficiently

   2.2 Carry out the tasks according to the time plan

   2.3 Work safely and hygienically

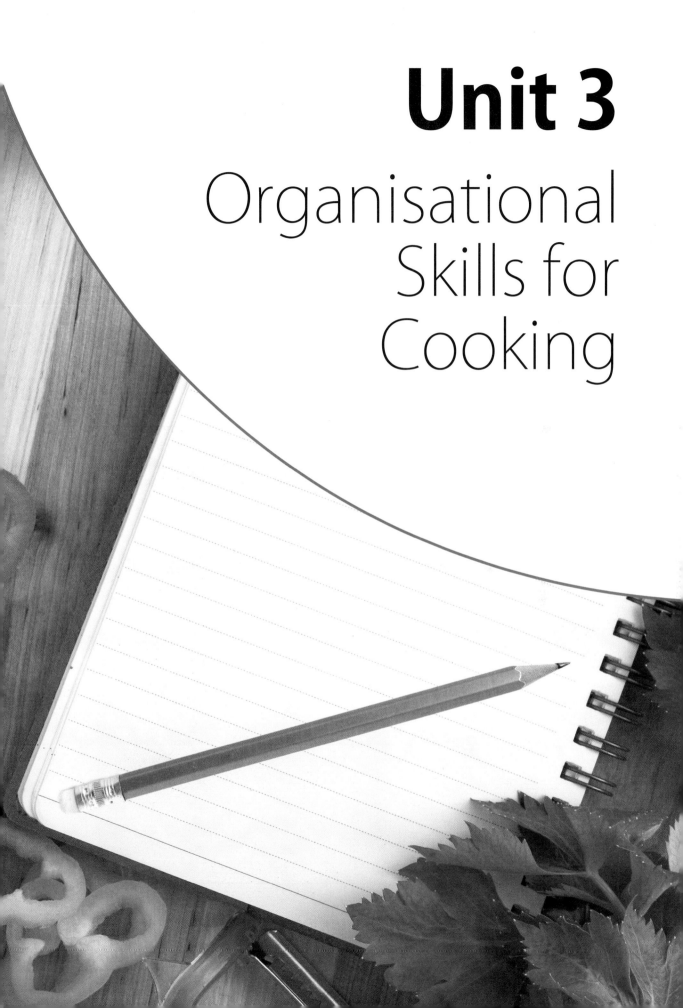

Unit 3

Organisational Skills for Cooking

5 Cooking up a complement

By the end of this chapter you should be able to:

- Select suitable recipes for a main course and a complementary starter or dessert.
- Prepare the dishes according to the recipes.
- Evaluate the prepared dishes in terms of presentation, taste and texture.
- Work safely and hygienically.

🔍 Hint

Waiting staff should be aware of the ingredients present in every dish, so that they can answer any questions the customers might ask.

Topic 1: Crack the combination

What does a chef have to consider when planning menus?

The head chef is responsible for selecting the dishes for the menu and deciding on how often to change it. They also have to decide on whether to offer any additional dishes on a 'specials' menu board, what these dishes will be, and how long the specials will be available. Head chefs are in control of the portion sizes of each dish and the price of them on the menu. There are, however, many other considerations they have to take into account.

Chefs use specials boards to show dishes that do not appear on the regular menu.

What does a chef consider when planning a menu?

The number of healthy choices on the menu
This is especially important if the restaurant is hoping to achieve the HealthyLiving Award – refer back to Chapter 3 Topic 2 for more details.

The balance of the menu
Does it offer a balance of nutrition, flavour and texture?

The space, equipment and skills of the staff
Only dishes that the kitchen can comfortably produce should be chosen.

Food allergies
The most common food allergies are to milk, eggs, fish, shellfish and nuts, so these items must be easy for the customer to identify on the menu. If a customer has not given prior warning of an allergy, the chef will have to be able to adapt or prepare a dish on the spot.

Food preferences
It would be impossible to cope with everyone's likes and dislikes but if there is a range of dishes, e.g. vegetarian, then there would be something for everyone. Special dietary requirements, e.g. fat free diets, may also have to be catered for.

Menu theme
Will the dishes have to highlight a special occasion or a particular type of cuisine, e.g. Italian?

Sustainability
What foods can be sourced all year round to prevent having to change the main menu.

Seasonality
What foods are in season and available locally as buying seasonal/local produce will help to keep the menu costs down.

A menu usually has a range of dishes on offer to customers, which allows them to make their own choice of starter, main course and dessert.

As part of this unit, you will have to select a main course and either a starter or dessert that complements the main choice.

🔍 Hint

Restaurants/hotels sometimes offer a set menu with either no choice or a very limited choice of two or three dishes for each course. This is usually a preferred option for large functions, such as a wedding, as it helps the chefs prepare in advance for the number of covers at the event. It also allows the chef to offer a more competitive price.

Considerations when choosing your two dishes

Firstly you will have to think about the following points, however don't forget to consider some of the points a chef makes when choosing a menu.

Flavour combination?
Choose a range of flavours which go well together.

Texture combination?
Choose more than one texture e.g. soft, crunchy, chewy.

My skills?
Think of the skills involved and whether you will be able to prepare them in the time allowed.

Presentation?
Think of how the finished two dishes will look when served-- will they look colourful and appealing? Will the dishes complement each other?

Reasonably healthy?
Check that the overall combination of dishes is not too high in fat, sugar or salt.

🔍 Hint

Try not to repeat flavours, e.g. Sweet and Sour Chicken contains pineapple, so don't serve it with a pineapple dessert.

When you have considered all these points, ask yourself, 'Would I like to eat the two dishes I have chosen?'

Topic 2: Rate your plate

Making food for other people can be a difficult task to get right. The way it looks and tastes is very important. As part of this unit you have to evaluate the presentation, taste and texture of the dishes you make.

What does evaluate mean?

Evaluate

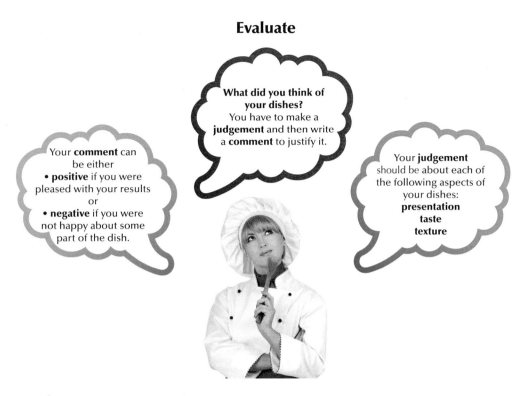

What did you think of your dishes?
You have to make a **judgement** and then write a **comment** to justify it.

Your **comment** can be either
• **positive** if you were pleased with your results
or
• **negative** if you were not happy about some part of the dish.

Your **judgement** should be about each of the following aspects of your dishes:
presentation
taste
texture

Presentation

This is the visual impact your dish will make.

- Serve on **clean**, attractive plates that complement the food.
- The dish should be served **hot or cold** according to the recipe and on the right temperature of plates.
- The dish should have a good **colour** depending on what you are making, e.g. if the dish has a grilled topping then it should be an even golden-brown colour.
- The **garnish/decoration** should enhance the appearance of the dish.

Here are some questions to ask yourself about the presentation of your dish:

Is it attractive/colourful – if so, in what way and why?

Is there a good contrast of colours on the plate?

Is the dish evenly browned?

Is it burnt because of over-cooking?

Is it too pale in colour?

Does it look neatly served?

Is the garnish neat? Is it appropriate?

Are the plates clean?

Are the plates the right temperature?

Taste

Always choose good-quality, fresh ingredients to give your dishes the best taste. A chef's tip is to always taste the dishes you are making **during cooking** and **before serving** to ensure your results have a good flavour.

Salt and pepper are the most commonly used seasoning, however, there are other many other ways of adding flavour to food.

- **Cooking liquids:** using stock, broth or wine instead of water for stewing, poaching, or making soups.
- **Adding a tangy flavour:** lemon juice, vinegar and wine all contribute acid to a dish, which livens up flavours and helps balance and complement sweet flavours.
- **Butter:** using butter will give a more creamy and rich flavour to cakes and biscuits than margarine.
- **Spices and herbs:** this helps to add flavour and helps to reduce the amount of salt required.
- **Adding a pinch of sugar** to tomato-based sauces helps to reduce the tanginess, giving it a more mellow flavour.

> **Some taste words that you can use when evaluating your dish are**: acidic, bitter, bland, buttery, mild, rich, salty, savoury, sharp, sour, spicy, strong, sweet, tangy, tasteless, mellow.

Texture

The texture of a food describes how it feels in your mouth. The texture of the food also plays a part in whether we like it or not. The ingredients used plus the preparation and cooking processes involved in preparing a dish will affect the final texture.

- The texture of apples could be described as crunchy.
- The texture of soup could be described as being lumpy or smooth.
- The texture of a fruit smoothie may be smooth and creamy depending on the ingredients used and how finely puréed it is.

> 🔍 **Hint**
>
> Often texture is linked with consistency, e.g. the level of puréeing of a soup could be a very smooth consistency when passed through a sieve compared to just being blended with a hand blender.

> ❓ **Did you know?**
>
> The texture of food changes, depending upon the cookery process used, e.g. tough cuts of meat become more tender when slowly cooked in a sauce.

> **Some texture words that you can use when evaluating your dish are:** chewy, close, creamy, crisp, crumbly, crunchy, dry, firm, flaky, greasy, gritty, hard, heavy, juicy, light, lumpy, moist, open, tender, tough, runny, short, soft, soggy, solid, smooth, sticky, stodgy.

☑ Chef's test

Complete the following:

1. Think about the following snack: a glass of orange juice, a wedge of pizza, a mixed salad.
   Come up with at least twelve words to describe it.

2. Think about the following meal: sliced chicken in a white sauce, cauliflower and mashed potato.
   a) Comment on the colour and texture of this meal.
   b) Make changes to the meal to make it more appealing.

3. Explain the word 'texture'.

4. Explain two ways of ensuring your dish is well presented.

5. What is a chef's tip for getting the taste right?

👨‍🍳 Service chef!

Select and prepare the following dishes and think about the presentation.

1. One that has a variety of colours, e.g. pizza.

2. One that has different textures, e.g. Quiche Lorraine.

3. One that is smooth, e.g. a puréed soup such as Carrot and Courgette Soup.

GO! End of chapter activities

Activity 1

Working in pairs

Design a two-course meal that shows the use of at least **three different textures**.

1. Write up the recipes for both dishes.

2. Give details of the presentation for each dish.

3. List the textures in each of the dishes.

4. Make the dishes, then taste them.

5. Evaluate the textures:
   a) Were they what was expected?
   b) Did the textures in the dishes complement each other?

Activity 2

Working on your own

Create a recipe bookmark for chefs called *"Crack the combination"*. The bookmark should give chefs a reminder about what they must consider when planning menus.

(*continued*)

Activity 3

Working on your own

Make up a top tips poster for chefs entitled 'Rate your plate' to remind them what to check before service.

Activity 4

Working in pairs

Develop a pasta dish that uses something other than salt to flavour the pasta.

1. Decide on a recipe.

2. Make the recipe.

3. Carry out a taste test with others in the class.

4. Using the prompts in the writing frame below, write a minimum of 50 words to evaluate your dish.

> Was it good? Explain your answer.
> Would you change anything, and if so what?
> Overall, was your dish a success?

Rate Your Progress

How confident are you that you have achieved each of the following objectives?

Using the following key as a guide, give yourself a rating for each of the objectives below.

Rating	Explanation
1	Confident with the standard of my work.
2	Fairly confident with the standard of my work.
3	The majority of my work was satisfactory.
4	Require to do some further work.
5	Require a lot of work.

Objectives	Rating
Select suitable recipes for a main course and a complementary starter or dessert.	
Prepare the dishes according to the recipes.	
Evaluate the prepared dishes in terms of presentation, taste and texture.	
Work safely and hygienically.	

Looking at your ratings

Write down two next steps to 'unlocking' your knowledge of organizational skills for cooking.

6 On your marks, get set, go!

By the end of this chapter you should be able to:

- Select and cost suitable recipes for a main course and a complementary starter or dessert.
- Prepare the dishes according to the recipes.
- Evaluate the prepared dishes in terms of presentation, taste and texture.
- Requisition the equipment and ingredients and organise the work area efficiently.
- Carry out the tasks according to the time plan.
- Work safely and hygienically.

Topic 1: Ready, steady, go

As part of this unit you have to select and prepare a main dish and either a starter or a dessert.

You will be given a range of dishes to choose from, so remember to select two dishes that complement each other. Also make sure you have chosen dishes that you have the confidence and skills to prepare on your own.

You have selected the following two recipes.

1. Main: Chicken Lasagne.
2. Dessert: Fruit Cheesecake.

Recipe 1: Chicken Lasagne
Ingredients

Chicken Sauce
Onion 50 g (prepared weight)
Green pepper 50 g (prepared weight)
Garlic 5 ml
Carrot 100 g (prepared weight)
Mushrooms 25 g
Chicken breast 125 g
Tomato puree 15 ml
Canned chopped tomatoes 100 ml
Chicken stock 100 ml
Dried basil 1·25 ml
Oil 15 ml

Cheese Sauce
Margarine 25 g
Plain flour 25 g
Semi-skimmed milk 300 ml
Mature cheddar cheese 50 g
Salt and pepper

Other Ingredients
Lasagne sheets 4
Garnish

Method

Chicken sauce.

1. Wipe/wash and slice the mushrooms.
2. Wash and deseed the green pepper. Cut into even-sized dice 5×5mm (macedoine).
3. Wash, peel and rewash the carrot. Cut into even-sized dice 5×5mm (macedoine).
4. Peel and finely dice the onion.
5. Peel and finely chop the garlic.
6. Make up the stock in a jug.
7. Add the tinned tomatoes, tomato purée and basil to the jug.
8. Cut the chicken into bite-sized pieces.
9. Heat the oil and fry the chicken and the chopped garlic until the chicken is sealed.
10. Add the onion, carrot, green pepper and mushrooms. Cook for 1 minute.
11. Add the ingredients from the jug and bring to the boil.
12. Simmer for 15 minutes until the chicken is cooked and the vegetables are tender. Taste and season as required.
13. Heat the oven to Gas Mark 6, 200°C.

Cheese sauce

14. Place the margarine, milk and flour in a pan.
15. Bring to the boil, stirring all the time and simmer gently for 1 minute.
16. Add 2/3 of the grated cheese and mix. Taste and season as required.
17. Place half of the chicken sauce in a dish, cover with two sheets of lasagne and half of the cheese sauce. Repeat these layers again.
18. Sprinkle the remaining 1/3 of grated cheese evenly over the top of the lasagne.
19. Bake for 15–20 minutes until ready and the lasagne is golden-brown in colour.
20. Garnish and serve.

Recipe 2: Fruit Cheesecake		
Ingredients		
Base margarine 50 g crushed digestive biscuits 100 g 	**Filling** cream cheese 75 g caster sugar 25 g thick-set raspberry yoghurt 100 ml whipping/double cream 125 ml	**Decoration** whipping/double cream 50 ml raspberries or other appropriate decoration

(continued)

Method

Base

1. Crush the biscuits.
2. Melt the margarine in a pan and mix in the crushed biscuits.
3. Press the mixture into a 15-cm flan ring, on a plate or up-turned baking tray, and chill.

Filling

4. Place the cream cheese and sugar into a large bowl. Beat them together very **lightly** with a wooden spoon until just mixed. (Do not over beat or it will be too soft.)
5. Gently mix in yoghurt to the cream cheese and sugar mixture.
6. Whip up all the cream (175 ml) in a separate bowl until stiff and standing in peaks.
7. **Remove two tablespoons** and place into a piping bag to decorate the cheesecake (place in fridge until required).
8. Carefully fold in the rest of the cream to the yoghurt mixture.
9. Pour mixture over biscuit base, smooth with a palette knife and place in the fridge to set.

Serving

10. Remove flan ring.
11. Using a fish slice, lift the cheesecake onto the serving plate using a fish slice.
12. Pipe with the remaining cream and decorate.

Note: an alternative flavour of thick-set yoghurt with an appropriate decoration can be used instead of raspberry.

Step 1: Ordering

You need to requisition (order) the ingredients you need for both dishes, then complete the following table for each recipe.

You must also order any **garnishes** or **decorations** you need.

	Equipment required
Recipe 1	
Recipe 2	
Garnishes and/or decorations	

> 🔍 **Hint**
>
> These two dishes complement each other with regard to flavour, texture and colour.

Step 2: Costing

Costing of recipes is important in the catering industry. A head chef will work out how many portions of each dish is needed and the cost of the ingredients required to make them. The head chef will also have to take into account other overheads such as:

- linen (napkins/tablecloths)
- staffing (e.g. waitresses, kitchen porters)
- fuel (e.g. cooking, heating, lighting)
- cleaning materials

Taking into account all of the expenses, the individual price per portion can then be worked out and a final price for the dish can be set.

Chefs should take into account the availability of ingredients and the foods that are in season and available locally, as this will help them keep the costs down.

What you have to do to work out the cost

Use the following formula to calculate the cost of each ingredient in both dishes you have selected (salt, pepper and garnishes do not need to be costed).

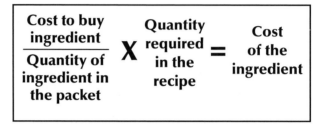

$$\frac{\text{Cost to buy ingredient}}{\text{Quantity of ingredient in the packet}} \times \frac{\text{Quantity required in the recipe}}{} = \frac{\text{Cost of the ingredient}}{}$$

🔍 **Hint**

Up-to-date prices can be obtained from most supermarket websites or your school may have a costing sheet.

Example: 100g of caster sugar is needed in a recipe

$\frac{£1.08}{1000g} \times 100g = £0.11$ **11p is the cost**

Note that figures should be rounded up (from 0.5p) or down to the nearest whole number.

Recipe 1			Recipe 2		
Ingredient	Quantity	Cost	Ingredient	Quantity	Cost
Total Cost			Total Cost		

Step 3: Time plan

If a restaurant is to be successful, **good planning** and **time management** are essential: but **why**?

Customers will be happy with the service, enjoy their meal and be more relaxed

Staff will be less stressed, able to cope if things go wrong and happy at their work

Before you start your time plan, you will be given a basic sequence of steps like the one shown below. This provides an outline of the activities you have to do in the time and it should be used as a guide to complete your own time plan

Hint

The outline plan is based on 100 minutes.

Start time: 9·15am **Finish time:** 10·55am (100 minutes)
Before you start, and throughout the task, carry out the following: • Safe and hygienic practices.   • Organisation of work station – collect ingredients.   • Set oven temperature.

Step	Time allowed	Activities
1		Base of cheesecake
2		Chicken sauce
3		Cheesecake filling
4		Cheese Sauce and chicken sauce
5		Assemble lasagne
6		Decorate cheese cake
7		Serving and finishing

Using the basic sequence of steps, for each step you should complete:
- the activities you will carry out to prepare and cook the two recipes
- the time you will take to complete each step.

Hint

Your timings should be in blocks of 10–15 minutes.

Hint

Remember the 5 Ps: **Prior Preparation Prevents Poor Performance.**

Remember that you have to include:

- testing for readiness
- tasting
- hygiene and safety points.

Here is an example of what a time plan could look like if you had 100 minutes to complete the task. Remember you will be able to do some prior preparation before starting to cook, for example grating cheese and weighing out ingredients. You would not need to include these tasks in your time plan.

Time plan (100 minute allocation)		
Start time: 9.15am	**Finish Time:** 10.55am	
Before you start, and throughout the task, carry out the following: • Safe and hygienic practices. • Organisation of work station – collect ingredients. • Set oven temperature.		
Step	**Time allowed**	**Activities**
1	9.15–9.25	**Base of cheesecake** Crush the biscuits. Melt the margarine, add the biscuit and mix. Press the mixture into the 15 cm flan ring. Chill in fridge. Wash up.

2	9.25–9.40	**Chicken sauce**
		Wash and prepare the vegetables.
		Make the tomato/stock mixture.
		Make the chicken sauce
		   – 5 mins to make
		   – 15 mins to cook
		   – Ready at approx. 9.55am
		Wash hands before and after handling chicken.

3	9.40–9.50	**Cheesecake filling** Start to prepare the cheesecake filling (see step 4 of recipe)
	9.50–10.05	**Cheesecake filling and chicken sauce** Check chicken sauce, taste for seasoning. Complete the filling and spoon over biscuit base. Place in fridge. Wash up.
4	10.05–10.15	**Cheese sauce** Make the all-in-one sauce. Complete the sauce – taste for seasoning.

(continued)

Step	Time allowed	Activities
5	10.15–10.30	**Assemble lasagne** Layer the lasagne (see step 17 of recipe). Sprinkle with cheese and place in oven for 15 minutes (ready approx. 10.45 am). Wash up.
6	10.30–10.40	**Decorate cheesecake** Pipe with the reserved cream and decorate with fruit ready for serving. Return to fridge until ready to serve.
7	10.40–10.55	**Serving and finishing** Wash dishes and unit. Check lasagne for readiness. Garnish. Serve both dishes.

Step 4: Preparing

Now it is time to prepare your dishes. Remember to:

- Organise your work area before starting and keep it organised as your work.
- Adopt a '**clean as you go**' approach. Do not let your dishes build up.
- Complete the tasks in order of your time plan and follow the recipes.
- Work safely throughout.
- Maintain a high standard of personal and kitchen hygiene throughout.
- Garnish your dishes before serving and make sure your plates are clean and at the right temperature before serving.

Stage 5: Evaluation

Evaluate the dishes in terms of:

- presentation
- taste
- texture

		Comment
Dish 1		
Presentation		The presentation of my lasagne was very good. The top was an even golden-brown colour and contrasted well with my parsley and tomato garnish.
Taste		The lasagne tasted good as the chicken sauce had a nice tomatoey taste, which went well with the cheese sauce.

> **🔎 Hint**
>
> You can remake part or all of a dish if something goes wrong. If you need to adjust your time plan, you can, without being penalised. You could take pictures of your finished dishes for your portfolio.

> **🔎 Hint**
>
> Start your evaluation by using some of these words to give an opinion of your dish: very good, good, satisfactory, could have been better, not very good, poor.
>
> Then you could use some of the words in Chapter 5 or words of your own to explain your opinion.
>
> Evaluate your dishes using each category in the table opposite. An example has been given for you.

(continued)

Texture	The texture was also good as the cheese sauce made the dish moist and the pasta was tender.
Dish 2	
Presentation	My cheesecake looked good as the raspberries and a mint leaf gave it colour.
Taste	The filling had a good taste as it was not too sweet and you could taste the raspberry flavour.
Texture	The texture was good with a crunchy base and a nice soft creamy filling.

Chef's test

Complete the following:

1. What do the 5Ps stand for?
2. Apart from the cost of the ingredients, list two factors a chef may consider when costing recipes.
3. Why should you adopt a 'clean as you go' approach during practical cookery?
4. What are the three aspects you should evaluate in a dish?

Portfolio

Make these dishes well and photograph them as evidence for your portfolio.

Service chef!

1. Select and prepare a starter and a main course to be served as part of a special meal for your grandmother's birthday.
2. Select and prepare a main course and a dessert to be served for a family tea.
3. Select and prepare a two-course meal for Sunday lunch.

End of chapter activities

Activity 1

Working on your own

Using the recipes for Chicken Lasagne and Fruit Cheesecake, draw up a time plan based on 2 × 50 minute periods in school. Refer to the time plan on page 153 to give you some ideas.

1. Decide on which preparations you can do beforehand.
2. Come up with a basic sequence of steps.

(continued)

Activity 2

Working on your own

A friend is coming to visit one evening and you are going to prepare a two-course meal.

1. From the recipes available, select a main course and a complementary starter or dessert.

2. List the equipment needed to make each recipe.

Recipe 1 Equipment	Recipe 2 Equipment

3. Cost the recipes. Note that figures should be rounded up (from 0.5p) or down to the nearest whole number.

Recipe 1			Recipe 2		
Ingredient	Quantity	Cost	Ingredient	Quantity	Cost
Total Cost			Total Cost		

4. Time plan. Either use the outline plan given to you or make your own time plan for the two dishes. Remember the time plan should not include all your prior preparation.

5. Evaluate the dishes. Write an evaluative comment for each of your dishes using the following headings.

Portfolio

Do Activity 2 well, as it could be kept for your portfolio of work.

	Evaluative comment
Dish 1	
Presentation	
Taste	
Texture	
Dish 2	
Presentation	
Taste	
Texture	

 Portfolio

Do Activity 3 well, as it could be kept for your portfolio of work.

Activity 3

Create your own two-course meal for 4 people that costs under £5 and uses at least one item of local produce.

If you have time, prepare and evaluate your meal.

Rate Your Progress

How confident are you that you have achieved each of the following objectives?

Using the following key as a guide, give yourself a rating for each of the objectives below.

Rating	Explanation
1	Confident with the standard of my work.
2	Fairly confident with the standard of my work.
3	The majority of my work was satisfactory.
4	Require to do some further work.
5	Require a lot of work.

Objectives	Rating
Select and use equipment to weigh and measure ingredients accurately.	
Apply a range of food preparation techniques using appropriate equipment with precision.	
Work safely and hygienically.	

Looking at your ratings

Write down two next steps to 'unlocking' your knowledge of understanding and using ingredients.

7 The final hurdle - reaching the finishing line

The aim of this section is to give you some pointers on how to do well in the course assessment.

National 5 Course Assessment Task

The Course assessment task for the National 5 Hospitality: Practical Cookery Course, is a practical activity. For this you will be given recipes (issued by the SQA), which you will use to plan, prepare and present the three given recipes.

The practical activity is worth 100 marks and consists of two stages:

Stage 1 – Planning – worth 15 marks

Stage 2 – Implementing – worth 85 marks.

All three dishes – a starter, main course and a dessert – have to be prepared in 2½ hours.

Stage 1 – planning

All your planning will be completed in a planning booklet, which is issued by SQA. This must be completed before you go onto Stage 2.

There are certain activities that you are allowed to do before starting the practical activity so **do not include** them in the time plan.

- You will be allowed to 'set up' your own personal work area with all the equipment needed for preparing, cooking and serving the foods.

- Weighing and measuring can be done in advance **unless** the recipe states 'prepared weight'. These ingredients must be weighed during the practical assignment as you get marks for correct weighing.

- If the recipe states that the ingredient can be prepared, e.g. 'peeled' onion/garlic/carrot, 'finely chopped' parsley, this shows you are allowed to do this in the preparation time. No other ingredients should be prepared.

- Garnishes or decorations can be prepared **unless** the recipe includes 'prepare garnish'.

? **Did you know?**

You are allowed to practise each of your dishes once in school, however, it is a good idea to also practise them at home. You should do this before you start your planning, as you can make notes on the recipe to help your timing, e.g. how long you took to do some of the skills and techniques. Try out some different garnishes/ decorations to help you decide on your final choice.

What you have to do

Task 1: Complete a time plan for the three given recipes **(9 marks)**. This will show how you intend to use the 2½ hours on the day of your practical activity to complete the three dishes issued by SQA.

Remember:

- Include starting and finishing times – you will be told these times.
- Time the activities into a minimum of 10-minute blocks.
- You don't have to write out each step of the recipe in detail, e.g. 'make pastry' is sufficient.
- Give timings of activities, e.g. preparation of ingredients such as vegetables, pastry etc.
- Cooking times – allow the correct length of time.
- Cooling/resting times. Include putting food into the refrigerator – this shows good food hygiene.
- Service times must be clearly indicated, e.g. starter – 2 hours after start time; main course – 2 hours 15 minutes after start time; dessert – 2 hours 25 minutes hours after start time.
- **To do well you should:**
  - include all the activities in the time plan
  - sequence them in the correct order
  - time them appropriately.
- **Remember to include safety and hygiene points in the time plan.**

  This could include:
  - washing hands at the start and at various points before and after handing foods, e.g. eggs, chicken
  - washing dishes as you go, and keeping you work area clean
  - washing vegetables
  - disposing of waste
  - storing perishable foods in the fridge
  - working safely when handling knives, equipment and cookers.

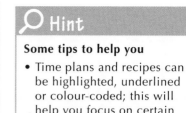

Don't forget to do a final check.

Are all the activities included?	✓
Have you included washing the dishes (wash as you go!)?	
Have you allowed enough time for preparing, chilling food in the fridge and cooking?	
Checking for readiness e.g. checking chicken/pasta?	
Heating your dishes?	
Tasting and seasoning?	
Time for garnishing and serving?	

Hint

Some tips to help you

• Time plans and recipes can be highlighted, underlined or colour-coded; this will help you focus on certain important activities or times, e.g. when to take a sponge out of the oven.

• Use a different colour for each course – starter, main course or dessert – this makes it even clearer.

Task 2: Complete service details for the three dishes (6 marks).

? Did you know?

It is a good idea to put the service times in first then work backwards from these to make sure your dishes have sufficient time to cook.

In this section you must detail how each of the dishes will be served. You must include the following:

• Temperature of service dishes – your recipe will tell you this.

• How the food will be presented – served individually or as a whole dish, and specific details of the type of serving dishes, e.g. in a soup tureen, in two separate serving dishes, on large individual plates.

• Details of the garnishes and decorations.

• Serving plates must be clean.

Hint

The garnish or decoration should not be overpowering. You will get additional marks for garnishing 'with flair'. This means you have to use a minimum of two components – e.g. a fruit coulis and a fresh fruit decoration – but also have a neat presentation overall.

It is important that the person marking your work is able to 'visualise' how your dish will look, so your service details must be clear. You can:

• give a written description or

• draw a labelled diagram of your service details.

Hint

Remember, when serving your dishes you must present them exactly as you have described in you plan or you will lose marks.

Look at the example given below:

Dessert:	Service time:
Service details:	
Serve on four individual clean plates at room temperature.	

Task 3: Preparation time

Before starting Stage 2 of the practical activity, you will be given time to do some preparations. This preparation time is important as it will allow you to get organised and be calm before you start.

Remember, these preparations should not be included in your time plan.

- Set up your work area with all the equipment you need.
- Weigh and measure all ingredients **unless** the recipe states 'prepared weight'. These ingredients **must** be weighed during the practical assignment in order to be awarded the marks.
- No ingredients should be prepared unless it tells you in the ingredient list, e.g. 'peeled' onion/garlic/carrot or 'finely chopped' parsley.
- Prepare garnishes or decorations **unless** the recipe tells you to prepare garnish as part of the method.

Stage 2 – implementing

You must prepare, cook, finish and serve the three dishes within the 2½ hours. Dishes served at the wrong time will not be awarded the marks available for service, although you will still be credited with any marks you have been awarded up to this point.

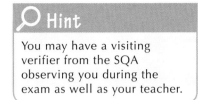

Your teacher will be observing you as you work, so it is important you do your best at all times. You will gain marks for everything you do correctly.

> **Hint**
>
> You may have a visiting verifier from the SQA observing you during the exam as well as your teacher.

How you are marked

Implementing the practical activity		
1. Skills/techniques/processes	**Mark allocation**	**Total**
Carrying out skills and techniques according to the given recipes	32–38	
Carrying out cookery processes according to the given recipes	8–12	
Presenting the dishes according to the service details	22–28	
The marks awarded to each of these three areas may vary depending on the three dishes given by SQA, but they will always total 70 marks.		70
2. Professional practice	**Mark allocation**	**Total**
Weighing and measuring ingredients	5	
Demonstrating hygienic working practices	5	
Demonstrating safe working practices	5	15
	Total marks	**85**

Skills/techniques/processes (70 marks)

- **Carry out skills and techniques accurately.**

  The assessment will always include vegetable preparation and cutting skills, e.g. slicing, finely chopping. It would be useful to make a list of all the other skills and techniques in

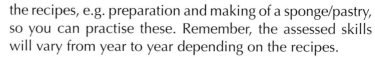

🔍 Hint

Put your hand up to let the person assessing you know when you are tasting.

the recipes, e.g. preparation and making of a sponge/pastry, so you can practise these. Remember, the assessed skills will vary from year to year depending on the recipes.

- Taste for seasoning.
- **Carry out the cookery processes** in the recipes correctly, for example:
  - Baking: make sure a sponge is baked correctly at the right temperature, and cake should be cooled slightly before being turned out.
  - Frying: make sure oil is at the correct temperature for frying; fry onion without discolouring.
  - Grilling: make sure the grill has been pre-heated.
  - Testing for readiness is essential during each of the cookery processes to ensure the food is cooked properly.
- **Service:**
  - Food and serving dishes must be clean and at the correct temperature.
  - Appearance: ensure correct colour, depending on the recipe.
  - Dishes should look the same as in the service details.
  - The dishes should be garnished or decorated appropriately, with flair where required.
  - Ensure good flavour.
  - Ensure correct texture/consistency.
  - There are a lot of marks to be gained for service of the finished dishes.

Professional practice (15 marks)

- **Weighing and measuring ingredients.** All ingredients identified in the recipe as 'prepared weight' are accurately weighed or measured, e.g. weigh the carrot after it has been diced.
- **Demonstrating hygienic working practices.** All tasks have been carried out showing a good standard of hygiene throughout the assignment:
  - **Personal hygiene:** jewellery, hair tied back and nail polish removed; protective clothing on; hands washed before starting, cuts covered.

    Remember you must wash your hands throughout the practical activity especially after handling raw meats and eggs.

- **Kitchen hygiene:**
  - taste food with a clean teaspoon
  - perishable food should be covered and stored in a refrigerator
  - separate chopping boards must be used for raw and cooked products
  - adopt a 'clean as you go' approach to your work – do not allow a large build up of dishes
- **Demonstrating safe working practices**. All tasks have been carried out with due regard to safe working practices, for example:
  - Handle sharp knives or equipment safely.
  - Use a damp cloth or paper towel under the chopping board so that the board does not move when chopping.
  - Assemble and use electrical equipment correctly.
  - Follow correct and safe oven procedures.
  - Ensure safe use of hobs, e.g. turn off when finished.
  - Use oven gloves.

> **? Did you know?**
> During practical work, touching your hair/skin, or coughing and sneezing over food, will lose you marks.

> **🔍 Hint**
> You could also practise other dishes with similar skills. This is similar to revising for other subjects and will help you achieve a better grade.

National 4 Added Value Unit

The Added Value Unit for the National 4 Hospitality: Practical Cookery Course, is a practical activity. For this you will follow a given time plan to prepare, cook, finish and serve a two-course meal, safely and hygienically, within 1½ hours.

The Added Value Unit is very similar to the practical activity at National 5. However, you are not awarded marks – it is a Pass or Fail result so do your best at all times! Lots of the information given for National 5 will apply also to National 4, so look back at the previous pages for more details.

The practical activity consists of **two** stages:

Stage 1: Planning	Stage 2: Implementing

You have to complete a planning booklet in which you must:
 	
• List the equipment you will need for both dishes.
• Provide service details of how you plan to serve your finished dishes. Your description should include:
  – the temperature of the serving plates
  – details of any garnish and/decoration.
 	
You can do this by:
 	
• giving a written description or
• drawing labelled diagrams of your service details.
 	
Whichever method you choose, the service details must be clear to allow the person marking your work to 'visualise' how your dish will be presented.
	You must prepare, cook, finish and serve both dishes within the 1½ hours.
	The teacher will be observing you as you work, so try to do your best at all times.
	
	• Weigh and measure ingredients accurately.
	• Prepare the ingredients as stated in the recipe – this could include using appropriate equipment and carrying out food preparation techniques to an acceptable standard.
	• Controlling the cookery processes – this could include adjusting the cookery process, e.g. adjusting the time/temperature of an oven when baking, testing for readiness etc.
	• You must taste your food for seasoning.
	• Serve and finish the dishes using garnishes or decorations.
	• Work safely and hygienically throughout.

 Hint

Tasting
When tasting food always use a clear spoon and never put the spoon back into the mixture without cleaning it first

Answers

Introduction

Starter for 10 answers

Countdown to 9. Get prepared

Chef's test

No answers required

Countdown to 8. How to become a rising star

Chef's test

1. Chef de cuisine', executive head chef

    Responsible for:

    – menu creation

    – management of kitchen staff

    – hygiene procedures

    – ordering and purchasing of inventory

    – plating design of dishes

2. The '*Sous-Chef* 's role

    – the second in command and direct assistant of the Head Chef.

    – scheduling and substituting when the Head Chef is off-duty.

    – filling in for or assisting the *Chef de Partie* when needed.

    – responsible for the inventory, cleanliness of the kitchen, organization and training of all employees.

3. Sections for Meat, Fish, Garnish, Larder and Pastry

Countdown to 7. Prevention is better than cure

Chef's test

1. No answers required

2. These are people who are employed by the government to protect public health.

They inspect food premises to make sure they are operating hygienically and are not a risk to public health.

They handle complaints about food quality, hygiene and safety issues.

Powers

Where they inspect a food premise and identify any potential risks they can:

1. Serve an improvement notice with a time scale for the work to be carried out

2. Seize foods samples and send them for testing

3. Serve an immediate closure notice

Countdown to 6. Keeping the bugs at bay

Chef's test

1. D) You can't tell. It looks, smells and tastes normal.

2. C) Fish, oysters and sushi

3. C) Dried, uncooked rice and pasta

4. B) 75°C or higher

5. **a)** storing raw meat above cooked meat in a refrigerator

    b) drying your hands on a tea towel

    c) not washing your hands after handling raw chicken

6. Cross contamination happens in when bacteria are transferred from their sources to a cooked food.

7. **a)** Indirect contamination.

    • licking fingers then handling food

    • using the same chopping board or knife for raw then cooked food

- using the same cloth after wiping a raw food area to wipe a cooked food area

b) Direct contamination.

- coughing onto food
- a fly landing on food
- blood from raw meat dripping onto the cooked meat below in a fridge

Countdown to 5. Watch your step

Chef's test

1. Items in a first Aid Box include:

- plasters, in a variety of different sizes and shapes
- small, medium and large sterile gauze dressings
- at least two sterile eye dressings
- crêpe rolled bandages
- safety pins
- disposable sterile gloves
- tweezers
- scissors
- alcohol-free cleansing wipes
- sticky tape
- cream or spray to relieve insect bites and stings
- antiseptic cream
- basic first aid manual

Any other suitable items may be included.

2 and **3** No answers required

Countdown to 4. Weighing and measuring

Chef's test

1.

Chilli Con Carne 4 portions
200g Mince 100g onion 200ml tinned chopped tomatoes 30ml Tomato Puree 150g Kidney Beans 10ml Chilli Powder 100ml beef stock. 150g Patna Rice

2.

Six dozen muffins
660 g butter 1500 g plain flour 1500 g caster sugar 12 eggs 750 ml milk 60 mls baking powder 1350 g fresh blueberries

Countdown to 1. Never a problem, only a solution

Chef's test

1. Throw it out and start again

   Before starting again make sure your hands are cool by running your wrists under cold water – this will cool the blood flowing into your hands/fingers.

2. The pasta is starting to over cook –

   Pour into a sieve, rinse with boiling water then stir in a little olive oil

   The cheese sauce is too thick –

   Add a little more milk to make it the correct consistency

   The top of the dish is not browning well and you are running out of time. –

   Place under a hot grill to brown or turn the oven up

3. Stir in a little more cold cream or whole milk if it is just starting to go beyond piping

   consistency – do not beat the mixture

   Throw it out and start again if it has started to turn to butter

4. Before baking:

   Dampen the pastry (with water) round the hole or on the sides and seal with a piece of pastry. Flatten into shape.

   After baking:

   If there is a hole in the pastry after baking, plug with a little left-over pastry (only if the hole is not too big and the flan case is to be cooked further) Small cracks – brush with a little egg to seal it.

Chapter 1 Tools and you

Topic 1: Cut it, page 38

1. Vegetable knife and Chef's knife.
2. No answers required.
3. Flat edged steels are preferred by many chefs as they are less likely to damage the blade of the knife during sharpening.
4. Red for the raw meat. Brown for the vegetables.

Topic 2: Bake it, page 45

1. **Balloon whisk** – Many chefs do not like using a hand-held electric whisk for whipping cream as it is very easy to over-whip the cream. They prefer to use a balloon whisk instead.
2. **Balloon whisk** – The most common shape is that of a wide teardrop, termed a balloon whisk. They are best suited to mixing in bowls, as their curved edges conform to a bowl's concave sides. **Flat whisk**, sometimes referred to as a roux whisk, has the loops arranged in a flat successive pattern. It is useful for working in shallow-sided pans and bowls. **Ball whisks** have no loops. Instead, a group of individual wires comes out of the handle, each tipped with a metal ball making it good for reaching into the corners of straight-sided pans. This whisk is easier to clean than traditional looped varieties.

3. A chinois is a conical sieve with an extremely fine mesh. It is used to strain custards, purées, soups, and sauces, producing a very smooth texture.

Topic 3: Cook it, page 47

1. Four points a chef should consider:

Points to consider	Explanation
Easy to clean	If not non-stick, the pans need to be easy for the staff to clean to save time.
Oven safe	The design and construction of the handles is important to ensure that they do not get too hot while in use.
Non-stick	This type of finish is beneficial for some tasks such as omelette making. Care must be taken, however, as the finish can be easily damaged.
Even heat distribution	The base should give even heat distribution to prevent any 'hot spots'.
Compatiblity	They should be able to be used with all types of cookers including induction hobs.

2. No answers needed.
3. They are easy to clean food does not stick to them

Topic 4: Serve it – all in the finish, page 50

1. No answers needed.

2. Chocolate run-outs or more intricate piping.

3. Cream, buttercream, chocolate, creamed potato, dough – choux pastry.

Chapter 2 Cookery skills, techniques and processes

Topic 1: Food preparation techniques, page 57

1. **Mix** means to combine ingredients evenly with a spoon or mixer.

   Blend is to combine two or more ingredients together to form a paste, usually a starchy powder with a liquid.

2. **Brunoise** – very small dice 2×2×2 mm. **Macedoine** – small cubed dice 3x3x3 mm (or 5x5x5 mm).

3. **Segmenting** is the process of removing the skin, for example from citrus fruits, then dividing the flesh into natural wedges.

4. Over handling will make the pastry tough.

Topic 2: Turn the heat up, page 65

1. A wet method of cooking involves using a liquid, for example boiling, poaching, steaming, stewing.

   A dry method of cookery does not involve the use of a liquid, for example baking, grilling, barbecuing, shallow frying.

2. The liquid used to cook the food in is often referred to as the cooking medium.

3. Stewing, as it is a longer and slower process which makes the meat tender.

4. Poaching involves cooking foods gently just below boiling point (usually 73–93°C) in a liquid. It is important that food is monitored regularly and it is not boiled.

   Little or no movement from the cooking liquid is required as this prevents delicate foods such as eggs and fish breaking up.

5. Two from:

Method of cooking	Explanation
Baking	Loss of nutrients is minimal as the food is served as a whole – water soluble vitamins are not drained off. Fruit and vegetables such as apples and potatoes can be baked and no additional fat is required.
Grilling	Grilling allows fat to drip away from the food making it a healthier method of cooking. Lean or trimmed meat can be cooked this way, which also reduces the fat content. No additional fat is usually required when grilling, however, a little oil may be sprayed or brushed onto the food to prevent it drying out.
Shallow frying	Shallow-frying is a quick method of cooking using a little oil. This helps to retain the nutrients.
Boiling	Boiling does not involve the use of fat.
Poaching	The cooking medium in poaching is generally water but stock, milk or wine may be used so no additional fat is used.
Steaming	Steaming is a healthy method of cooking as no fat is needed and there is little loss of nutrients because the food is not directly in the water.
Stewing	Serving the liquid helps to retain nutrients that may have leached out of the food into the liquid during the cooking process.

Topic 3: Testing for readiness, page 68

1. By using a knife - a thin bladed knife should pass easily through the thickest part.

   By sight – the flesh of the skin should be opaque. If it is translucent it is not cooked.

   The flesh of the fish should 'flake' or come away easily from the bone.

2. Cream turns to butter.

3. Cakes should be golden-brown and spring back when the surface is pressed lightly with the fingertips. The cake should also be starting to shrink back from the sides of the tin.

Topic 4: All in the finish, page 75

1. A **garnish** is used on a savoury dish. A **decoration** is used on a sweet dish.

2. As follows:

   a) Remove a slice from the top and the bottom of the orange – this provides a flat base to start.

   b) Cut the outer skin from the flesh, working from the top to the bottom. It is important to follow the natural shape of the orange and to remove only the outer skin and pith without removing excess flesh of the orange.

   c) Remove any remaining pith before cutting out each segment between the inner membranes.

3. Three from:

   a) **Grated**: Use a block of chocolate that is cold and firm and use a hand grater. It is a good idea to cut the chocolate up into smaller blocks for grating as this will prevent it from melting in the hands before being grated. It is also advisable to thoroughly wash and dry the grater surface at regular intervals as the chocolate will not grate properly if the blades become coated in chocolate.

   b) **Curls**: To make chocolate curls, use a vegetable peeler with a long narrow blade. Warm the blade and chocolate slightly then use the peeler to peel along the smooth surface of the chocolate to make curls.

   c) **Melted:** Melted chocolate can be used to give swirls, drizzles, curls and chocolate shapes. To cut out shapes, smooth the melted chocolate over a piece of parchment paper. When the chocolate is just about set but still flexible, use cutters to make the desired shapes such as leaves, circles, hearts. Leave the chocolate shapes to completely set before removing from the parchment paper for use.

   d) **Chocolate run-outs**: To make chocolate run-outs make a paper piping bag first and fill with the melted chocolate. Snip the piping end with sharp scissors then pipe shapes onto parchment paper. Allow to set completely before removing.

4. • Put the parsley bunch in a bowl of cold water and swish it around; dirt will fall to the bottom of the bowl.

   • Remove parsley from bowl and shake off excess water.

   • Place parsley on a clean paper towel and pat the parsley.

   • Carefully remove the leaves from the stem and remember only take off as much as you plan to use immediately.

   • Gather the leaves into a pile, and slice roughly. Remember to use a sharp knife as a blunt knife will bruise the leaves.

   • For a finer chop, use one hand to hold the tip of the knife on the cutting board while the other hand rocks the knife down and across the leaves.

   • Continue until the parsley reaches is the desired size.

5. A garnish/decoration should not only enhance the look of the dish but complement the flavour of the dish as well. Colour and texture can be added.

Chapter 3 Plate it up!

Topic 1: What's on your plate?, page 87

1. Any two from:

- Use herbs and spices to flavour foods instead of salt.
- Always taste food before adding salt. This can be during the cooking process or before serving.
- Provide reduced-salt versions of foods, for example baked beans, peas.
- Make your own stock using vegetables or use lower in salt stock cubes.
- Limit the use of soy sauce or change to low-salt soy sauce for stir-frying.
- Offer 'salt substitute' as an option to salt.

2.

Nutrient	Effect on health
Protein	Protein is needed for • Growth of body cells. • Repair of body cells. • Maintenance of body cells. The secondary function of protein in the body is: • Energy Not enough protein: • Growth in children is slow. • Cuts and wounds will take longer to heal. Too much protein: • The protein can be converted to fat in the body. • This can lead to obesity if it is not used up as a secondary source of energy.
Iron	1. Iron is a component of haemoglobin, the substance that forms red blood cells. 2. Haemoglobin helps to transport oxygen around the body to every cell to help reduce the feeling of tiredness. 3. Iron is required to prevent anaemia. Not enough iron: • Tiredness, lacking in energy, weakness. • Anaemia.
Calcium	1. With phosphorus it combines to make calcium phosphate which gives hardness and strength to bones and teeth. 2. Required for the maintenance of bones and teeth. 3. Helps to prevent osteoporosis in later life. 4. Helps blood to clot after injury. 5. Required for the correct functioning of muscles and nerves. Not enough calcium: • Low intake over a period of time may lead to poor development of bones (leading to rickets and soft bones) and teeth (leading to dental caries). • If a bone is broken or damaged then it may take longer to heal if calcium is lacking. • Osteoporosis (brittle bones) in later life. • Osteomalacia (adult rickets). • Blood will not clot well after an injury.

(continued)

Nutrient	Effect on health
Folic acid	Folic acid is needed: • To make red blood cells and prevent a type of anaemia. • To ensure unborn babies grow and develop properly and helps protect against neural tube defects such as 'spina bifida' in unborn babies. Not enough folic acid: • A type of anaemia. • Babies are at risk of being born with spina bifida.
Vitamin C	Vitamin C is needed: 1. To make connective tissue to bind the body cells together. 2. To help cuts and wounds heal quicker. 3. To help protect the immune system. 4. To assist in the absorption of iron to prevent anaemia. 5. To build and maintain the skin. 6. Vitamin C is an anti-oxidant vitamin. Not enough vitamin C: • Cuts and wounds fail to heal properly. • Anaemia may develop as vitamin C has to be present to allow iron to be absorbed. • There is a greater risk of developing cancer and heart disease in later life as vitamin C is an anti-oxidant vitamin.
Vitamin A	Vitamin A is needed: 1. To assist in good vision particularly in dim light. 2. To keep the mucous membranes healthy. 3. For the maintenance of healthy skin. 4. For growth in children. Not enough vitamin A: • Vision in dim light is not so good. • Dry and infected skin and mucous membranes. Too much vitamin A • Can be harmful to the developing foetus during pregnancy.
Vitamin D	Vitamin D is needed: 1. For the proper formation of bones and teeth. 2. To promote quicker healing of bone fractures. 3. For the absorption of calcium and phosphorus. Not enough vitamin D: • Poor growth and a risk of rickets in children where bones become soft and bend. • Osteomalacia (adult rickets) in the elderly. • Osteoporosis – brittle bones – where calcium will be lost from the bones.

3. Any five from:
   • Wholemeal varieties of breads, pitta breads, granary rolls and bagels should be available.
   • Potatoes should be baked or boiled with the skin on.
   • If potatoes are mashed use low fat spreads and skimmed milk.
   • Baked potato wedges are a healthier option than chips.
   • Where chips are on the menu, customers should also have the option of a healthier alternative such as baked or boiled potatoes.

- Serve rice boiled or steamed and use whole grain. Avoid fried rice such as pilau and egg fried rice.
- Add pasta or rice to soups to make them more filling.
- Serve pasta with tomato based sauces.

4. Any three from:

- Serve tomato or vegetable-based sauces with pasta instead of cheese sauce.
- Use a variety of vegetables in soups – soup can be liquidised to encourage children to eat it.

- Add extra vegetables to pizzas, spaghetti Bolognese or any other dish that is popular with children.
- Offer fresh fruit as a breakfast or as a dessert option.
- Smoothies are a good way of using a variety of fruit and are a good way of getting children to eat fruit.
- Add dried fruit such as apricots, cranberries, sultanas to baking, breakfast cereals and desserts.

5. Identify the main nutrients found in each section of the 'Eat Well Plate'.

Fruit and vegetables	Bread, rice, potatoes, pasta and other starchy foods	Meat, fish and alternatives and other non-dairy sources of protein
• Vitamins A, C, E • Iron • Vitamin B Vitamins including folic acid • Total complex carbohydrates	• Total Complex Carbohydrates • Calcium and iron • Vitamin B complex • Potatoes – are a source of vitamin C	• Protein • Vitamin B Complex • Iron • Oily fish will supply Vitamins A and D • Fish with bones are a source of calcium and phosphorous

Milk and dairy foods	Food and drinks high in fat and/or sugar	
• Protein • Calcium • Vitamins A and D	• Fat • Carbohydrates – sugar	

6.

Suggestions	Reasons
Change cooking apples to eating apples.	These will not need sugar to sweeten them.
Add dried fruit/ fresh raspberries and reduce sugar.	This will reduce the sugar content.
Change plain flour to a mix of wholemeal and white flours.	This will add more fibre.
Add some oatmeal or porridge oats to the topping.	This will add more fibre.
Change margarine to polyunsaturated margarine.	This will reduce the saturated fat content.
Reduce the amount of sugar in the topping.	This will reduce the sugar content of the dish.

7. No answers required.

Topic 2: Eating out, page 91

1. • The customer might choose to eat at a restaurant which has achieved a healthyliving award as it shows that they are serving healthier food and helping their customers make better food choices.

   • It makes it easier for customers to eat healthier food when eating out especially someone who has an interest in health/ on a weight reduction diet/ has special dietary needs, e.g. reduced-salt intake.

2.

Lasagne	• Use lean minced beef. • Drain any fat off after browning. • Use turkey mince. • Use Quorn™ mince. • Use semi-skimmed or skimmed milk in the sauce. • Use a stronger flavoured cheese and reduce the quantity in the sauce.
Cheesecake	• Use lower in fat cream cheese. • Use reduced-fat cream or yoghurt in the filling.

3.

Ham sandwich made with white bread	• Change the white bread to wholemeal • Add salad, tomato, cucumber to the filling.
Spaghetti Bolognese	• Add more vegetables to the Bolognese sauce. • Use wholemeal pasta.
Cheese and Tomato Pizza	• Add more vegetables to the pizza topping, e.g. mushrooms, peppers, onions. • Use wholemeal flour in the pizza base.

4. No answers required.

Chapter 4 Get to know your ingredients

Topic 1: Meaty matters: meat and meat alternatives, page 100

1. To avoid contaminating other foods, store in the bottom of the refrigerator so no blood can drip onto other foods causing cross-contamination.

2. a) **Choosing:** choose lean or extra-lean versions of mince and steak for casseroles. Choose cuts of meat such as steaks that are lean with little visible fat.

   b) **Cooking:** Drain fat off from meat either after it has been browned or skim off the fat on the surface after it has cooled. Brown meats in non-stick pans or use cooking sprays. Choose a method of cookery where no additional fat is added e.g. stewing, grilling.

3. Roast beef – horseradish sauce, gravy, Yorkshire puddings; roast lamb – mint sauce, gravy, redcurrant jelly;
   roast pork – apple sauce, gravy, sage and onion stuffing.

4.

Meat alternative	Storage	Current dietary advice
Soya beans – TVP	• Easy to store for several months as it is dried – needs no special storage conditions. • Frozen varieties need to be stored in the freezer until required.	• Low in fat. • A good source of protein. • It contains some dietary fibre. • It is low in calories. • It is fortified with amounts of iron, vitamin B complex and in particular vitamin B_{12}.
Tofu	• Store in the refrigerator. • Left-over tofu should be put in a dish and covered in water. Cover the dish and it will now stay fresh in the fridge for up to 3 or 4 days. The water should be changed daily.	• A good source of protein. • Low in fat. • Contains calcium.
Myco protein - Quorn ™	• Frozen Quorn™ needs to be stored in the freezer. • Fresh Quorn™ should be stored in the refrigerator.	• Low in fat. • Low in calories. • Contains protein. • A source of dietary fibre. • Provides zinc and vitamin B complex.

5.

Cut of meat	Method of cooking	Recipes
Rump	• Stir frying • Grilling	• Stir fried beef • Warm rump Steak salad
Sirloin	• Grilling (steak) • Roasting (whole)	• steak with mushroom and wine sauce • Stroganoff
Topside	• Roasting	• Roast beef with trimmings • Roast ginger Scotch beef with sweet potato salad

Topic 2: The chicken run - poultry and poultry alternatives, page 102

1. Poultry should always be covered with foil/cling film or sealed in a plastic bag before storing at the bottom of the refrigerator to prevent any of the juices coming into contact with other foods in the fridge. The cross-contamination caused by bacteria such as *Salmonella* and *Campylobacter* and increases the risk of food poisoning.

2.

Preparing	To lower the fat the skin could be removed before cooking or buy skinless chicken breasts.
Cooking	Roasting poultry. Place the poultry on a rack in the roasting pan so that the fat drips away during cooking. Cooking chicken with the skin on will keep the chicken more moist but the skin should be removed before eating. Choose a method of cookery where no additional fat is added, e.g. in a stew/casserole, grilling/stir frying.

3. **Roast turkey** – cranberry sauce, gravy, bread sauce, sausagemeat/oatmeal stuffing;

   roast duck – orange sauce/cherry sauce, gravy, sage and onion stuffing;

   roast goose – apple sauce/sage and onion stuffing.

4. No answers required.

Topic 3: A fishy tale – fish and seafood, page 104

1. **a)** Omega 3 is found in various concentrations in many different kinds of seafood. It comes from the family of 'good' fats that are not only beneficial for health but that are essential in the diet. These fats cannot be made by the body, so a dietary supplement is essential.

   b) Omega 3 has been linked with:
   - brain development in unborn babies and young children
   - reducing the chances of developing diseases such as cancer and heart disease
   - joint function
   - healthy skin and eyes
   - better mental health

2. Any two from:
   - They can eat most types of fish and shellfish when pregnant – there are only a few types to limit or avoid.
   - It is recommended that they eat at least two portions of fish each week, one of which should be oil-rich (a source of Omega-3).
   - There is no need to limit the amount of white fish or shellfish eaten when pregnant, apart from shark, swordfish and marlin.
   - Limit the amount of tuna to no more than two fresh tuna steaks or four medium-size cans of tuna a week. This is because these fish can contain more mercury than other types of fish, which could affect the baby's developing nervous system.
   - During pregnancy there is an increased need for Omega 3 – oily fish is an important source of this.
   - There is no need for pregnant women to miss out on shellfish, as long as they ensure it is thoroughly cooked.

3. Any two from:
   - They are a good source of protein, which will help growth and repair of tissues.
   - White fish is low in fat so will help prevent weight gain.
   - Oily fish such as salmon will supply Omega 3, which will help brain development in unborn babies and young children and help reduce the chances of developing diseases such as cancer and heart disease.
   - Vitamin A helps night vision and is an anti-oxidant vitamin so helps prevent cancers and heart disease.
   - Vitamin D helps the absorption of calcium and so aids the development of strong bones and teeth.
   - Fish where the bones are eaten, e.g. tinned salmon or sardines, are good sources of calcium and phosphorous so helping the development and maintenance of strong bones and teeth.

4. Rinse in cold water, dry and loosely wrap in foil or cling film before storing in the refrigerator.

   Store it away from foods such as milk which will absorb the smell of the fish and use within 24 hours.

   Fresh fish can also be frozen if it is not to be cooked on the day it is bought.

Topic 4: From the farm: dairy products and dairy alternatives, page 109

1. Cheese

a) Holland, e.g. Gouda, Edam.

b) France, e.g. Camembert, Brie, Roquefort, Boursin.

c) Italy, e.g. Ricotta, Mascarpone, Gorgonzola, Mozzarella, Parmigiano-Reggiano (parmesan), Pecorino.

d) Switzerland, e.g. Emmental, Gruyère.

e) Germany, e.g. Allgäuer, Emmentaler, Bavarian Blu, Tilsiter.

f) Scotland, e.g. Dunlop, Caboc, Crowdie, Lanark Blue, Cheddar.

2. Milk

a) UHT, e.g. sauces, custard, items of baking.

b) Semi-skimmed, e.g. with breakfast cereals, sauces, baking.

c) Dried, e.g. items of baking such as scones, bread.

3. For storage either reseal the cheese in the original package or wrap in clingfilm/tinfoil/plastic food bag and keep in the refrigerator.

4. Cream.

Cream	Use
Single cream	It is used to give richness to some dishes, e.g. curries/soups and to serve with desserts.
Whipping cream	Can be whipped for filling, e.g. choux pastries, meringues or as a topping on desserts.
Double cream	Similar uses to whipping cream.

Cream	Use
UHT or long-life cream	Single cream – can be poured over desserts, added to soups. Double cream – can be whipped and used to top desserts.
Clotted cream	Usually served with scones and jam.
Crème fraîche	Used as a topping on desserts or added to soups. A low fat version is available.

5. Helps the digestive system.

Topic 5: Let's get cracking! – eggs, page 111

1. a) Coagulation: When an egg is added to a combination of ingredients, the protein coagulates when heated. Used for binding ingredients together, coating and thickening.

b) Lightening: Eggs trap air when whisked or beaten, e.g. meringues, whisked sponges. Egg white traps more air then a whole beaten egg.

2. a) Scotch Eggs, fish in breadcrumbs, potato croquettes.

b) Hamburgers, fishcakes.

c) Rice pudding, scones, mashed potatoes.

3. Any two from:

- Keep eggs refrigerated after purchase.
- Store blunt end uppermost so that the yolk is surrounded by the white. This helps to keep the egg fresh.
- Store away from strong-smelling food – egg shells are porous.
- Make sure you use eggs by the 'best before' date shown on the egg or box.

4. Duck, goose, quail.

5. When hard boiling eggs it is important to run the egg under cool water as soon as it is cooked, otherwise the iron will combine with the sulphur in the egg and form a black ring round the yolk, which will make the egg look less appealing.

Topic 6: Take the pledge! – fruit and vegetables

1. One from each section.

Selecting	• Buy as fresh as possible. • Avoid bruised or wrinkled fruit and vegetables. • Ready prepared produce will have reduced vitamin C due to advanced preparation and storage. • Frozen vegetables will have a higher vitamin C content as they are frozen quickly after being picked.
Preparing	• Avoid soaking as vitamin C is water soluble and will leach out into the water. • Do not prepare in advance as vitamin C will be lost through oxidation. • Knives should be sharp as blunt knives cause more cells to be damaged, resulting in loss of vitamin C. • Avoid peeling if possible or peel thinly as most vitamin C is just under the skin.
Using	• Cook vegetables immediately after preparing. • Add to boiling water and cook for as short a time as possible. • Use as little water as possible for cooking. • Choose short methods of cooking, e.g. steaming, microwaving or stir-frying.

2. Any one from:

Fruit	Fact
Pineapple	• Pineapples have a cylindrical shape, a scaly green, brown or yellow skin and a crown of spiny, blue-green leaves and fibrous yellow flesh. • Areas that grow pineapples include Hawaii, Thailand, the Philippines, China, Brazil and Mexico.
Mango	• This is a tropical fruit wth yellow/light orange and a flavour similar to apricots and pineapple. • Mango originates in the Far East.
Kiwi fruit	• Originally called a Chinese gooseberry this fruit was renamed to kiwi fruit, in honour of the native bird of New Zealand, the kiwi, whose brown fuzzy coat resembled the skin of this fruit. • The green flesh has a fresh tangy flavour and has many small, black, edible seeds.
Bananas	• Bananas are sweet with firm and creamy flesh and are available for harvest throughout the year. • Bananas are thought to have originated in Malaysia around 4,000 years ago. Today, bananas grow in most tropical and subtropical regions including Costa Rica, Mexico, Ecuador and Brazil.

3. Fruit and vegetables are sources of:

- Vitamins A, C ,E which are anti-oxidant vitamins.
- Green vegetables and dried fruit contain iron.
- Some vegetables contain B vitamins including folic acid.
- They are low in calories.
- Almost all are fat-free.
- They also are a good source of fibre, especially if the skins are eaten.

4.

Raspberries	Raspberries are best kept in the refrigerator.
Potatoes	Potatoes should be kept in racks or in paper bags in a cool, dark, well-ventilated place.
Cabbage	Should be kept in the refrigerator or cold store.

5. Fresh fruit juice, fruit smoothies, fruit yoghurts, grilled tomatoes, lightly sautéed mushrooms.

Topic 7: In the store cupboard – dry ingredients, page 122

1. Spaghetti, penne, lasagne sheets, tagliatelle, cannelloni, fusilli, farfalle, macaroni, fettuccine, ravioli, tortellini.

2. Pasta is made from durum wheat, a variety of strong flour, which is ground into a fine semolina. The semolina is mixed with water or egg to make a paste. This is then forced through a machine into many different shapes such as penne, spaghetti or sheets of lasagne. The formed dough is then dried under controlled conditions. Fresh pasta can also be produced.

3. Sugar:

Sugar	Use
Demerara	Can be sprinkled on top of a dessert, e.g. crème brulée, which can then be grilled to give a crisp topping.
Icing	Can be used for icings and sprinkled for decoration.
Granulated	A general all-purpose sugar used to sweeten, for example hot drinks, stewed fruit.
Caster	It is used for creaming cakes, whisked sponges and meringues.

4. a) Gluten is the protein substance found in strong flour.

   b) When the flour is mixed with liquid, the gluten stretches due to the bubbles of gas produced in the dough by the raising agent (yeast) and forms the risen structure of the bread during cooking.

   c) Coeliacs.

5. Whole grain breakfast cereals are the best. They are usually fortified with a range of minerals such as iron, vitamins such as the B group and D. They are also a good source of fibre.

6. Fortification means that additional nutrients have been added, e.g. breakfast cereals, flour, bread, fruit juice, etc.

Topic 8: Spice it up! – herbs, spices, flavourings, seasonings, page 128

1.

Fresh	Fresh growing herbs should be kept in a cool place and the soil should be kept moist. Many supermarkets sell pre-cut fresh herbs in sealed bags, which require refrigeration after purchase.
Dried	Dried herbs should be stored in an airtight container.

2. Mono sodium glutamate. Some people are allergic to MSG and products containing MSG are high in salt so could increase the risk of high blood pressure.

3. Pepper:

Black pepper	It can be added to almost every savoury dish, hot or cold, giving a sharp and strong flavour. Black pepper will show up as black specks, so is best used in dishes where this would not be noticed, e.g. tomato-based dishes.
White pepper	Light-coloured sauces or mashed potatoes, where black pepper would show as black specks.
Mixed peppercorns	This is ground down and used to flavour savoury dishes that would be flavoured with black pepper.

4. Any three from:

- Always store spices in an airtight container and place them in a dark area such as a cupboard.
- Spices should be kept away from moisture, sunlight and sources of heat, all of which damage the spices.
- Use by the best before date so that they retain their aroma and flavour.
- The containers must be properly resealed after use.

5. **Rock salt** is a coarse version of the finely ground table salt. Its coarse texture makes it easy to pick up and sprinkle on food during or after cooking. It can also be used in a salt mill at the table. Sea salt is produced by evaporating salt water collected from an ocean or sea.

Sea salt is less refined than other salt. Depending on the seawater used, there is also a variety of minerals in the sea salt but only in very small amounts. Chefs believe that sea salt has a better texture and flavour than ordinary table salt. It can be used in a salt mill at the table.

Topic 9: Sustainable food, page 131

1. No answers required.

2. Sustainability is about finding ways of providing foods that are accessible throughout the year and have less of an impact on the environment. Chefs have to consider sustainability when planning menus to ensure the required ingredients are continually available.

3. Two from:

- It is a good way to buy in-season foods at their freshest and possibly save money.
- Farmer's market stalls will often have samples of local produce to taste before you buy.
- Buying produce direct from a farm should also mean tastier and fresher produce. Boxes contain a selection of in-season vegetables, fruit, meat, and fresh eggs to order.
- Some farms will offer organic produce which is useful for people who are concerned for the environment or who have allergies.
- Locally grown produce can be delivered direct to the door or a restaurant. This can help to cut down on shopping trips, saves time and fuel emissions, helping to create a cleaner environment.
- Fresh fruit and vegetables may not come wrapped in plastic when bought locally, and this helps to reduce packaging waste and pollution.

4. Food miles is the distance that food travels from 'field to plate' (the journey from where food is grown or produced to the consumer).

Food miles make us aware of the effect on the environment that transporting food around the world causes, i.e. increased greenhouse gas emissions. Growing concern over carbon emissions has led to the growth of the number of consumers who would prefer to eat only 'locally' grown food rather than food that has travelled many 'food miles'.

Chapter 5 Cooking up a complement

Topic 1: Crack the combination, page 145

1. No answers required.

2. **a)** Colour – Lacking in colour, pale, white looking. Texture – soft, lacks crispness, no crunch.
   b) Sauce – add mushrooms for colour and texture. Change cauliflower to carrot batons, broccoli for more colour. Mashed potatoes – change to a baked potato or potato wedges with spice – more texture and colour.

3. Texture is a description of how a food feels in your mouth.

4. Any two from:

   serve on clean, attractive plates that complement the food. The dish should be served hot or cold according to the recipe.

The appearance – the dish should have a good colour depending on the dish, e.g. if the dish has a topping then it should be an even golden-brown colour.

The garnish/decoration should enhance the appearance of the dish.

5. Always taste the dishes you are making during cooking and before serving to ensure your results have a good flavour. Always choose good-quality, fresh ingredients to give dishes the best taste.

Chapter 6 On your marks, get set, go

Topic 1: Ready, steady, go, page 154

1. **P**rior **P**reparation **P**revents **P**oor **P**erformance.

2. How many portions of each dish is needed; linen (napkins/tablecloths), staffing (waitresses, kitchen porters, etc.), fuel (cooking, heating, lighting), cleaning materials.

3. To prevent the dishes building up.

   To keep the worktop tidy.

   To prevent cross contamination.

4. The three aspects are: Presentation, taste and texture.